AN INTRODUCTION TO

WINDSURFING

AN INTRODUCTION TO WINDSURFING

Light Wave

Light Wave

Light Wave

THE
APPLE
PRESS

ACKNOWLEDGEMENTS

The author wishes to thank Sola Wetsuits,
Hyjumpers, Super Surf Ltd., Lightwave, Paul
Davies, Kathy Myres and David Buckland for their
help in compiling this book.

A QUINTET BOOK

This edition published 1989 by
The Apple Press
6 Blundell Street
London N7 9BH

ISBN 1 85076 170 1

This book was designed and produced by
Quintet Publishing Limited
6 Blundell Street
London N7

Art Director: Peter Bridgewater
Designer: Ian Hunt
Editors: Julie O'Rouke, Shaun Barrington
Photographer: Alex Williams
Additional photographs: Philip Holden,
(page 10 and 58, top right)
Illustrator: Rob Schone

Typeset in Great Britain by
Central Southern Typesetters,
Eastbourne
Manufactured in Hong Kong by
Regent Publishing Services Limited
Printed in Hong Kong by
Leefung-Asco Printers Limited

Contents

Whether you sail on inland waters or brave the high winds and big waves of the open sea, windsurfing is sailing in its most elementary — and some would argue most enjoyable — form. There are few more direct ways of competing against, or of collaborating with wind and water — and the secret is definitely out! Over the last few years the sport of windsurfing has expanded worldwide at an astonishing rate. Millions of people now own boards and many more have tried their hand at the sport either by renting or borrowing equipment while on holiday. To cope with this demand, a handful of major manufacturers produce boards by the thousand, mainly aimed at the beginner's end of the market. There are also a number of small firms producing specialized high performance boards for professional and progressive sailors.

Windsurfing has grown in popularity so quickly that most people tend to see it as a sport that has sprung up almost overnight. However, the first sailboard can be traced back to 1965 when an American, S. Newman Derby, published an unpatented design that was similar in principle to today's craft. The first practical board is credited to an aeronautical engineer named Jim Drake. Between 1967 and 1968 Drake worked on two "free sailing systems" in which a rubber universal joint enabled the board to be steered by rig-movement alone. Drake teamed up with a Californian entrepreneur named Hoyle Schweitzer and together they resolved the initial teething problems inherent in the design. By the end of 1968 a US patent was applied for in order to protect the invention of the aptly named "windsurfer". Schweitzer, regarded by many as the father of the sport, continued to develop prototypes until he arrived at a design very similar to the boards of today. Having acquired

The Board and Rig

1 Nose or bow. Sometimes fitted with a rubber bumper and towing eye.
2 Tail or stern.
3 Skeg or fin. Used singularly, or in triangular formations.
4 Retractable daggerboard. Sometimes made to retract into the hull.
5 Footstraps. Fitted in several configurations.
6 Mast foot well. Often allowing two positions. An alternative is a sliding mast track (6a).
7 Daggerboard well. Reinforced and built into the hull.
8 Mast or spar. Made from fibreglass or aluminium, with a single or double taper.
9 Mast foot and universal joint. Made to lock into well, or release under tension.
10 Boom or wishbone. Fixed or variable length. Modern booms tend to be shorter than the one illustrated.
11 Sail clew. Reinforced with metal eyelet.
12 Outhaul. Sometimes used with a pulley system, and tied off with a cleat on the boom.
13 Boom front end. Often with grip handle.
14 Inhaul. Tied off with a cleat.
15 Uphaul. Knotted to give grip. Hawaiian type is soft with elasticated core.

16 Shock-cord. For use with regular uphaul.
17 Downhaul. Sometimes used with a pulley system, and tied off with a cleat on the mast foot.
18 Safety cord. Joins the mast foot to the board.
19 Battens. Fitted into batten pockets. Battens are now often secured by batten tensioners, buckles or loops which close off the end of the batten pocket.
20 Leech of the sail.
21 Foot of the sail.
22 Luff of the sail.
23 Mast sleeve.
24 Head of the sail.
25 Mast head.
26 Class insignia.
27 Tack of the sail.

Plan view (above) The positioning of the footstraps, mast wells, and daggerboard case, is a primary consideration in board manufacture.

Left A typical funboard and rig in the Maui sunshine of Hawaii.

Far left Board and sailor in perfect harmony.

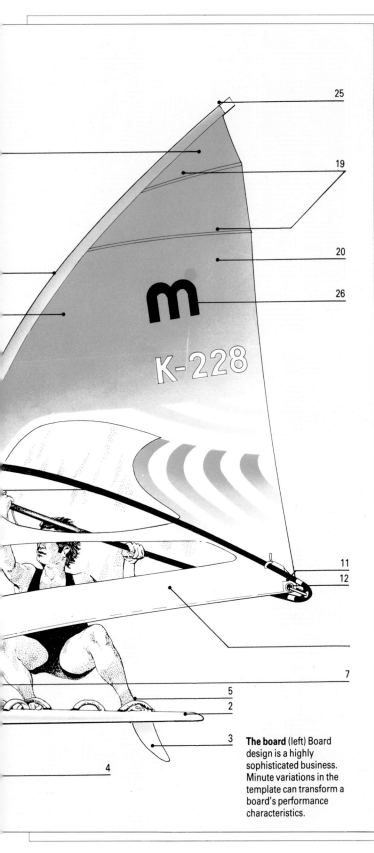

The board (left) Board design is a highly sophisticated business. Minute variations in the template can transform a board's performance characteristics.

Drake's half of the patent, Schweitzer started to manufacture a small number of complete "windsurfers" and subsequently used all his available resources to take out patents in as many countries as possible. This proved to be a shrewd move as before long a few large European concerns began to produce increasing quantities of sailboards. As is the case with many patented products, legal wrangles developed over claims as to who actually invented the windsurfer. Eventually, after lengthy court proceedings, the majority of large manufacturers agreed to honour Schweitzer's seven and a half per cent royalty fee.

The wrangle over the UK patent recently took a new turn when in 1984 an Englishman named Chilvers claimed that in 1958 as a schoolboy, *he* had produced a free-sailing system. Although crude, Chilvers' sailboard was in fact recognized under British law as the first of its kind. The patent became invalid in Britain and similar decisions followed in the courts of other countries, thus stimulating the already buoyant windsurfing trade.

The technical development of windsurfing continued at an accelerating pace throughout the 1970s. Most boards, however, remained similar to Schweitzer's "Windsurfer One Design". These large, stable boards came to be known as flatboards, a term based very obviously upon their appearance. Racing on flatboards became very popular, usually around a triangle course which tested the speed of the board and the all-round ability of the sailor.

Although the flatboard was an ideal learning apparatus, keen racers and competitive manufacturers soon arrived at a faster hull shape which offered increased performance potential — but at the expense of stability and ease of sailing. The development process led to a rounded hull section incorporating an

It is simple to understand why a flat board is so named. The flat hull and large immersed surface area — ensuring stability — are its great assets and make it ideal for the beginner.

Although in plan view the Division II board appears similar to the flat board its rounded hull-section makes it as easy to balance on as a log!

The allround funboard is an ideal learner's board. It is advisable in the early stages to remove the footstraps as they will only get in the way.

extremely high volume (300–350 litres). These characteristics gave increased speed and efficiency for sailing to windward — the most critical aspect of the dinghy-style triangle racing adopted by windsurfers. With the birth of this new style of board it became necessary to separate fleets for racing purposes. The flatboards were to sail in Division I, and the rounded boards in Division II. Division I thus became identified with leisure racing and Division II with more serious, professional racing, a situation which still exists today — although both Divisions are very competitive.

While racing in the traditional I and II Divisions quickly gained popularity, a new breed of windsurfer had also begun to emerge. These sailors were more interested in competing against the wind and water than against other sailors. This new system of sailing was funboarding, a style developed in the excellent surf conditions of Hawaii. Its starting point was the development of footstraps in the mid seventies. Footstraps are exactly what they sound like — straps for the feet — and they served two purposes: they kept the sailor firmly attached to the board while going out in surf or high wind and they also enabled him or her to steer the board with the feet or more correctly, to steer by foot pressure. This brought about a higher degree of board manoeuvrability. As sailors progressed, boards were streamlined for extreme performance in extreme conditions, and Hawaii became overnight the centre of windsurfing research and development. With consistent testing in warm climates and strong wind, the so-called funboard sailors progressed rapidly. Highly visual photographs from Hawaiian shores soon made funboarding and its superstars the envy of all recreational sailors.

The long funboards (around 3 metres 70 cm/12 feet) available today are still based on the original flatboards, but with increased performance in a

Turning a sinker.

wider range of conditions. With similar volume (220–250 litres) and hull shape to the flat board, all-round funboards make very good first-time boards. They are stable for beginners and hold a distinct advantage over the flatboard, in that once a sailor is proficient, he or she will not outgrow the equipment quite so quickly.

Today there is an extensive range of funboards which get progressively shorter in length. The ultimate in manoeuvrability and control is the *sinker*. As the term suggests, due to its low volume the board sinks under the rider's weight when not in motion. Often under 2 metres 70 cm (9 feet) in length, sinkers are ideal for wave-sailing and high speed. Their major drawback is that they will not plane in winds of less than 20 knots. With the quality of equipment and teaching methods now available a novice can make quick progress in the early stages. Sailing in extreme conditions, however, takes a lot more practice, but at either end of the scale it is easy to experience the thrill offered by the sport. Once hooked, the future holds no limits!

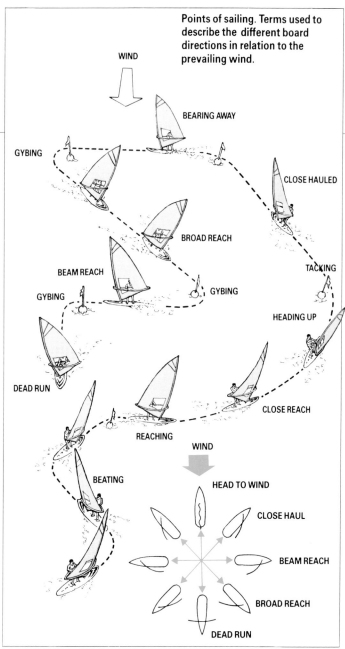

Points of sailing. Terms used to describe the different board directions in relation to the prevailing wind.

▶ SAILING TERMINOLOGY

Many a practical problem encountered by sailors of all standards can quite easily be explained, and eventually overcome, by sound theoretical knowledge.

In windsurfing, as in sailing, port and starboard are the terms used for the left- and right-hand sides of the board. The problem with "left" and "right" is that interpretation depends entirely on which direction the sailor is facing. Therefore port is always the left side of the board when looking from the stern towards the nose. Starboard is the right hand side as seen from the same point.

If the wind is blowing over the port side of the board, the board is said to be on a port tack, and the converse applies for starboard.

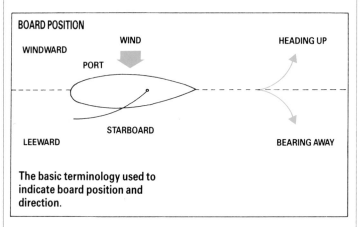

BOARD POSITION

The basic terminology used to indicate board position and direction.

Anything that is upwind of a given object is said to be *windward*, and anything downwind is said to be *leeward*.

Changing the course being sailed is again described in relation to the wind. To *bear away* or *bear off* is to steer the board onto a more downwind course. *Heading* or *luffing up* is taking a more upwind course.

The different directions sailed in relation to the wind are called the points of sailing.

Sailing directly across the wind is called *beam reaching*. If the board bears away and sails a diagonal course downwind, it is said to be on a *broader reaching* course. Sailing dead downwind is called *running*. A diagonally upwind course is the fine point of sailing called a *close-haul*.

Changing course from a port to starboard tack or vice versa can be achieved in only two ways. The first is turning the nose of the board through the eye of the wind. This process is called *tacking*. The second method involves the tail of the board passing through

the eye of the wind. The board is turned downwind, and the manoeuvre is called *gybing*.

▶ TRUE AND APPARENT WIND

Apparent wind is the wind caused by a combination of the *true wind* (the wind felt whilst stationary) and the wind coming from ahead which is created by the craft's forward motion.

It is to the *apparent wind* that the sailing craft actually sails, and it is therefore important to understand its characteristics. As a board's speed increases, the effect of the apparent wind is also increased. There are two elements to apparent wind, however, namely speed and direction. As board speed increases, so does the force of apparent wind. To clarify this, if you sail a straight course across the wind, with theoretical optimum sail-trim, you will note that as board

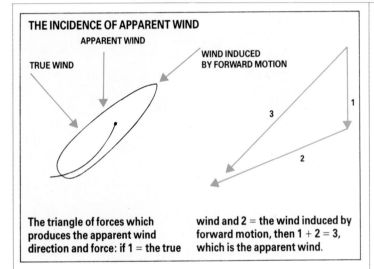

THE INCIDENCE OF APPARENT WIND

The triangle of forces which produces the apparent wind direction and force: if 1 = the true wind and 2 = the wind induced by forward motion, then 1 + 2 = 3, which is the apparent wind.

speed increases it will be possible to sheet in harder, yet still remain on the same course.

▶ *STEERING*

Basic steering is accomplished by moving the sail forwards and backwards in line with the sail's chord-line (i.e. along the centre line of the board when drawn from nose to tail). The effect of this is that the centre of effort in the sail (the point where the power of the wind is concentrated) will move in front of or behind the centre of lateral resistance of the board (i.e. the dagger board/skeg) which acts as its pivot point.

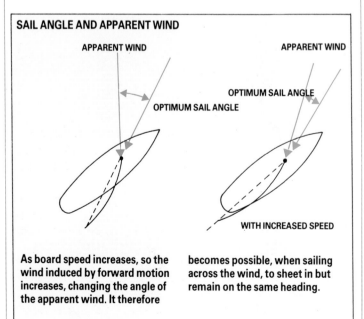

SAIL ANGLE AND APPARENT WIND

As board speed increases, so the wind induced by forward motion increases, changing the angle of the apparent wind. It therefore becomes possible, when sailing across the wind, to sheet in but remain on the same heading.

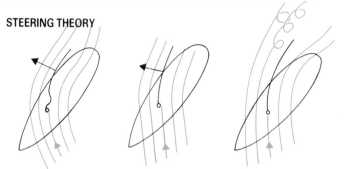

STEERING THEORY

Chord line angle The most efficient sailing position is where the sail's chord line is at an angle of 20° to the 'apparent wind'. If the angle is too small the sail will luff and the leeward airflow will lose contact in places, and reduce the pressure difference. If the angle is too great, the leeward airflow will be disturbed and the air leaving the sail will create turbulence.

Centre of effort A sailboard is steered by tilting the rig forwards and backwards. The 'centre of effort' (CE) is the point at which the main force of the wind acts on the sail. This force has a sideways effect, to counteract which it is necessary to have a daggerboard. The daggerboard is the 'centre of lateral resistance' (CR).
When the CE is vertically above the CR the board travels in a straight line. When the sail is tilted forward the CE moves forward and the CR acts as a pivot in the water, forcing the bow downwind. Conversely, as the sail is tilted back the CE goes vertically behind the CR and the stern is pushed to leeward, causing the board to luff up to windward.

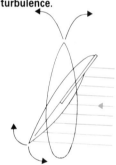

Heading up Tilting the rig backwards, causes the bow to turn up into the wind.

Bearing away Tilting the rig forwards, causes the bow to turn away from the wind.

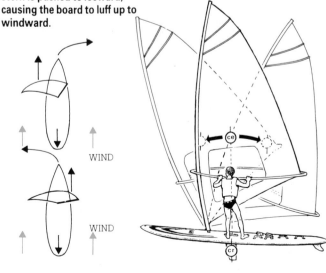

If the rig is angled back, the centre of effort (CE) moves behind the centre of lateral resistance (CLR); and the pressure in the sail will cause the board to "luff up" into the wind. If the rig is moved forward, the torque created by the CE being forward of the CLR means that the tail of the board moves upwind, and the board will correspondingly point further downwind. It follows that the extent of rig-movement will be directly related to the turning characteristics of the board. These turning characteristics can be easily affected by changing the angle of the pivot point, namely the daggerboard. This concept is particularly useful in stronger winds where the rig is raked back progressively in order to maintain control. Likewise the centre of effort also moves back. To prevent the board from luffing up, the daggerboard can be angled back to maintain equilibrium.

When the daggerboard is retracted fully, the skeg, and to some degree, the rails of the board act as the only restraint on the unwanted sideways movement of the board. Although these have far less effect than the daggerboard in reducing lateral movement, they nevertheless offer enough resistance when sailing on points off the wind. On the downwind course the centre of resistance in the rig is naturally further back because the sail is raked further back.

These basic principles can also be applied when sailing funboards in stronger winds. These boards do have different turning characteristics; with a daggerboard up, the board will turn in a similar fashion to a surf board or a water-ski. The steering principle here revolves around the angle of depression of the rail.

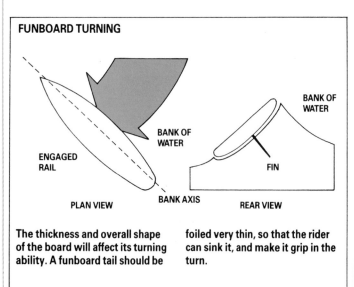

FUNBOARD TURNING

ENGAGED RAIL

BANK OF WATER

BANK OF WATER

FIN

BANK AXIS

PLAN VIEW

REAR VIEW

The thickness and overall shape of the board will affect its turning ability. A funboard tail should be foiled very thin, so that the rider can sink it, and make it grip in the turn.

Powering through the surf; always be wary of offshore winds in such conditions.

The characteristics of the turn are determined by many factors, including the velocity of the board, and the body-weight committed to the rail.

Boards with different tail-shapes and rail-profiles have their own turning characteristics. A rounded-profile rail, lower volume tail and vee in the rear section of the hull are factors that contribute to sharper turning. A board with a high-volume tail and flat underwater section will be more difficult to turn. Explaining the intricacies of board design would require a book in itself. Suffice to say here that although a board's performance characteristics will be influenced by the design, the basic principles of steering and control will be much more obvious to the novice than any design principle.

▶ THEORY OF SAIL POWER

The driving force necessary to propel the windsurfer forward is generated *totally* by the airflow which passes over the sail.

The fact that a windsurfer can sail directly down-wind is simply due to the sail-area acting as a resistance to the flow of air. The force in the sail is directed into the board as forward movement. The fact that a board can sail across the wind, or even diagonally upwind, is a slightly more complex phenomenon. Basically the sail behaves as a crude aerofoil. Airflow directed smoothly over its surface results in pressure-differences between the windward and the leeward sides. The pressure created on the leeward side is

lower than the windward pressure, giving rise to a suction effect which creates movement — an effect similar to that which keeps aircraft flying. The dagger board prevents the board from moving sideways and ensures that power is converted into forward motion.

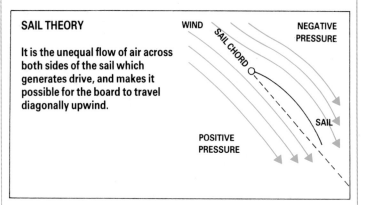

SAIL THEORY

It is the unequal flow of air across both sides of the sail which generates drive, and makes it possible for the board to travel diagonally upwind.

The total force of the sail is referred to as the resultant force. This is an effect of the lift generated by the sail and the drag-characteristics of the board in the water. This force is concentrated at the centre of effort in the sail, and has a definite direction and magnitude.

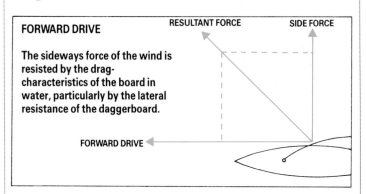

FORWARD DRIVE

The sideways force of the wind is resisted by the drag-characteristics of the board in water, particularly by the lateral resistance of the daggerboard.

The lateral resistance of the hull causes the resultant force to split into forward drive and side-force. All of the sail's force is transmitted to the board via the sailor and through the mast-foot. Since the force in the sail is constantly changing, due to differing wind-strengths and changes in board resistance on the water, the sailor must constantly alter his stance to maintain maximum use of the forces in the rig.

◄ Well-tuned equipment is easier to control in all situations.

► THE TRIM OF THE SAIL

A sail can be presented to the wind at many angles, the optimum angle usually being about 15°. In practice this angle can be found by sheeting in gently with the back hand until the sail begins to stall and the board begins to slow down. As this happens, sheet out a little until a maximum speed is achieved.

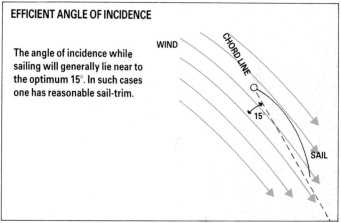

EFFICIENT ANGLE OF INCIDENCE

The angle of incidence while sailing will generally lie near to the optimum 15°. In such cases one has reasonable sail-trim.

The trim, actually the angle of incidence of the sail to the wind, is never 100 per cent perfect as there is always a time-lapse between changes in wind-direction and the sailor's ability to respond. The sailor also has to cope with the effects of the apparent wind. When the wind begins to swing round, the angle of incidence will naturally become less. To compensate for this, the sailor must sheet in to regain the optimum angle. In practice this is taken to extremes while speed-sailing, where a sailor may be broad-reaching in relation to the true wind, but is sheeted in to maintain trim in relation to the apparent wind. It is especially difficult to maintain trim in gusty conditions. Rarely do completely constant wind-conditions occur, and gusts and lulls often incorporate slight changes in wind-direction. The sail obviously needs trimming constantly to maintain the correct angle of incidence and therefore generate the most power.

To summarize, the angle of incidence is more variable in relation to the windsurfing rig than in other sailing craft. A windsurfing rig is, however, easiest to trim and compensate for, owing to the sailor's continual and direct contact with the sail. For the novice, sail-trimming may be something of an ordeal, as he or she has to be constantly aware of it. After a few months, however, trimming becomes almost natural. A sailor is then free to concentrate on the more exciting aspects of the sport.

Initial Techniques

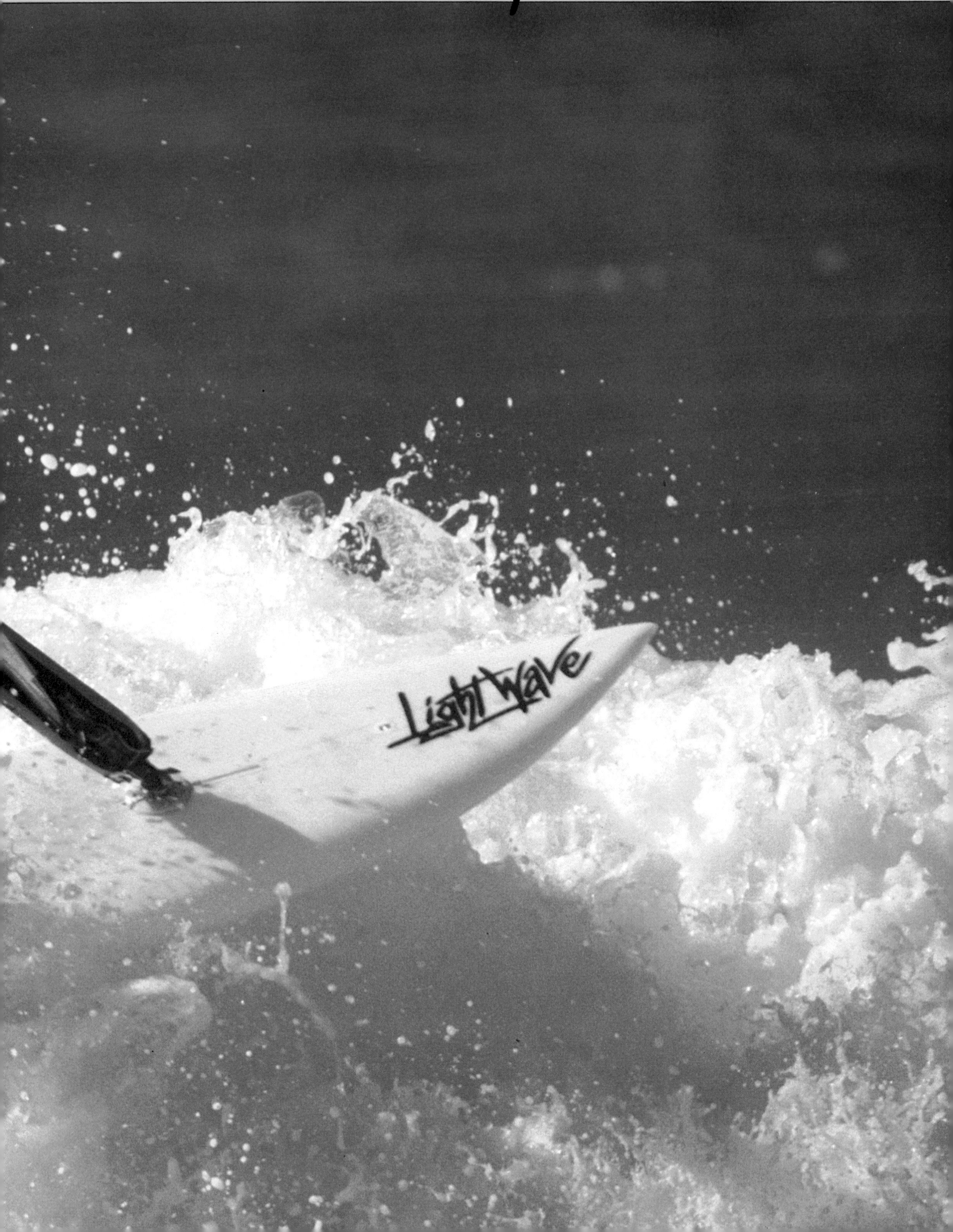

▶ LET'S RIG IT RIGHT

Rigging up in a hurry is a common misdemeanour committed by sailors of all abilities. Rigging is an integral part of windsurfing and if done incorrectly makes time spent on the water more difficult and possibly more dangerous than necessary. The essence of good rigging is to be methodical. There are no prizes awarded for being first on the water, and in the long run time is actually saved by careful rigging, as the rig will need little attention while in use.

Make sure you have all the bits and pieces close at hand. This is particularly important if rigging up some distance from your base, or your vehicle. Before starting the assembling process make sure that all components are in a good state of repair. Take special care to inspect the lines as they are prone to breakage under strain if damaged, leading to a potentially dangerous situation if one gives out while sailing.

▶ ATTACHING THE BOOM

There are various ways of attaching the boom to the mast. The method you choose will be primarily dictated by the type of front boom-end on your particular model of board. As all manoeuvres are initiated with boom pressure, it is imperative that the mast/boom connection is really firm in order to maintain full control.

▶ CLOVE-HITCH METHOD

Lashing the boom to the mast with a clove-hitch already fastened to the mast is a method possible with nearly all boom ends.

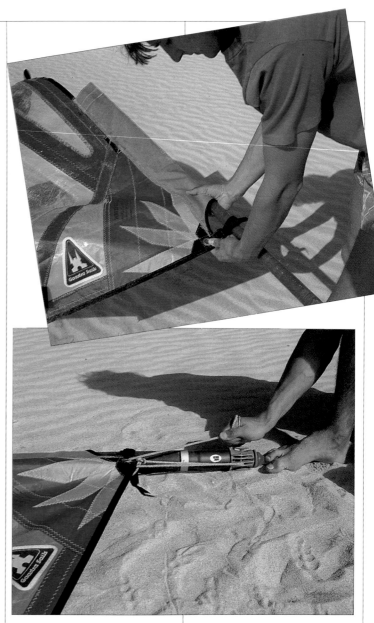

TYING A CLOVE HITCH

The clove-hitch is simple and quick to tie. It is used to lash the boom to the mast.

1 Unroll the sail and insert the thin end of the mast into the luff-tube. To aid insertion it may be necessary to slightly withdraw any battens. Be sure the mast tip reaches the end of the luff-sleeve.

Take the mast foot and slide it into the base of the mast. The mast foot should be a close fit so take care to remove any grit or sand from either the foot itself or from inside the mast otherwise the mast foot will be reluctant to come out when de-rigging afterwards.

2 Secure the downhaul to the mast foot through the eyelet in the foot of the sail. Enough tension is now required to secure the mast-foot, so thread the downhaul through the cringle and apply slight tension. A bowline is the correct nautical knot to tie the downhaul to the cringle. If you were not in the Guides or Scouts, a few half-hitches will suffice. For comfort while sailing, it is important that the boom is set at the correct height. Initially, up-end the mast.

3 To check the correct boom height, stand next to the mast. An individual's boom height is really a matter of personal preference. As a guide, shoulder-height is the norm. This method of checking boom-height should not be used in high winds!

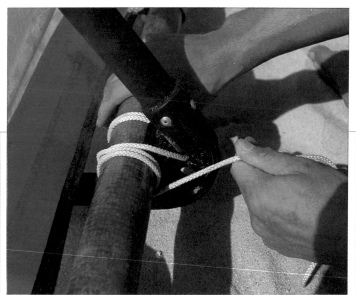

1 The inhaul line consists of approximately one and half metres of pre-stretched rope with a knot at one end. This is attached to the mast at the required boom-height using one of the simpler knots in the sailor's repertoire, namely the clove-hitch.
Place the boom over the mast and the sail into its sailing position below but adjacent to the clove-hitch.

2 *Top right* Holding the boom firmly against the mast, pass the inhaul line down through the front boom end and wrap the line twice around the mast below the boom.

3 Proceed to feed the inhaul back up through the boom end and wrap it around the mast above the boom. Now tie the remainder of the inhaul securely off using at least one half-hitch. If the boom has a cleat, use it but still finish off with the half-hitch.

4 The boom should now be firmly fixed to the mast. To test for a good fitting hold the rig upright. The boom should stay in its sailing position, although as yet it has no outhaul supporting it.

▶ QUICK-FIT SYSTEM

If you have a modern boom, the chances are that it can be fitted quickly and firmly by a quick-fit system which is usually incorporated into the front boom end. Boom ends tend to use different quick-fit systems but the principles are similar; a series of holes and cleats is nearly always used. The illustrated example is one of the most common methods.

If the boom tightens up excessively during this process, stop levering! The boom may crack the mast. Return the boom to its position along the line of the mast and slacken the inhaul off slightly. Only now proceed to lever again. A tight connection can then be achieved without undue strain on the mast. Repeat this adjusting process as many times as required. Always lever the boom upwards to increase tension. Apart from being easier as there is less interference

1 Position the boom along the line of the mast. The rear boom end will be in close proximity to the mast foot. In this instance the inhaul is already connected to the front boom end forming a small loop at source.

2 Take the inhaul and pass it twice around the mast at the correct boom height, maintaining the small loop. Direct the line up through a hole opposite the line's anchor point and immediately back down through the nearest hole.

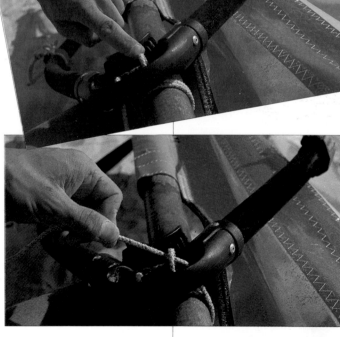

3 *Above* Once again, pass round the mast. Pass the inhaul up a hole next to the small loop. Direct the line under the loop and pull firmly. Twisting the mast as you pull should tighten things up.

4 *Right* Gently lever the whole boom from the rear end upwards towards the clew. Take care not to trap the luff sleeve in the jaws of the boom end.

from the sail and battens, doing so will mean that force exerted while sailing will relieve pressure on the mast, rather than increase it.

▶ FINAL TOUCHES

Once confident of a solid mast/boom connection, turn your attention to the clew area of the sail. The outhaul must be tensioned to a point where the clew is close to the rear boom end (provided the boom is the correct length for the sail). To help you here, most booms incorporate integral pulleys and cleats in the rear end fitting. This makes lighter work of out-hauling.

When the outhaul and downhaul tensions are correct the battens can be fully tensioned. The rig should appear almost perfect. It is usual however to fine-tune the sail by a combination of slight outhaul and down-haul movements. In light airs the sail should be tuned so that its profile is full. As the wind increases, the profile should get progressively flatter. Remember that in strong airs the required increase in out-haul tension will need a corresponding increase in downhaul. Obviously when a sailor finds himself struggling to make a flat-set sail still flatter, it is time for him to change down to a smaller sized sail.

▶ INCORRECT RIGGING DIAGNOSIS

Anyone with relatively little rigging experience will find it all too easy to rig up incorrectly. However, any problem can soon be rectified as the cause is often fairly easy to spot. The most common problems are a loosely fitting boom, or insufficient outhaul, down-haul or batten tension.

1 *Top right* If you're feeling a little weak while outhauling, it may help to sit down and use your foot against the boom in order to pull the rope.

2 Return to the mast-foot for final downhaul adjustment. Brace your foot against the mast-base and pull for all you're worth. Modern sails do require heavy downhaul tension. When the sail is downhauled correctly, there should be deck clearance of 20–25 cms/8–10 ins.

3 Finally, view the rig with wind in the sail. If the rig feels comfortable and looks good, the odds are that it is set correctly for the prevailing conditions.

1 The *boom to mast connection* is a common bugbear among the windsurfing fraternity. It is imperative that the connection be firm to attain definitive control. If you find that the boom is working loose before or during sailing, there is nothing for it but to start again from square one. If you are on the water this means sailing back to the shore. Needless to say, you should not attempt to de-rig at sea. Ease off downhaul tension and completely release outhaul tension. Reconnect the mast to the boom and proceed to re-rig with care.

2 Horizontal wrinkles indicate the need for more increased *downhaul tension.* A pulley mechanism may help to increase tension. If pulleys are not available thread the downhaul several times between the cringle and mast-foot to attain a crude but similar purchase-ratio. It is very difficult to overdo the downhaul tension, but if the luff-area appears excessively flat then ease off tension a little.

3 *Below right* The outhaul setting is critical for the handling of your rig. *Insufficient outhaul* will make control very difficult as the sail's centre of effort will shift fore and aft in response to the slightest change in wind-strength.
If the sail appears baggy, or maintains vertical creases when full of wind, more outhaul is required.
Unlike the downhaul, it is a common mistake to over-tension the outhaul. The sail will be visibly flat and consequently be underpowered in use. In this case, ease off tension until a profile reappears in the sail.

4 *Bottom Insufficient batten tension* is indicated by numerous small vertical wrinkles along the batten pocket. More tension may be achieved by the use of modern slotted batten end-caps. With correct batten tension, continuity will appear in the sail-profile. Its laminar air-flow characteristics will be improved.

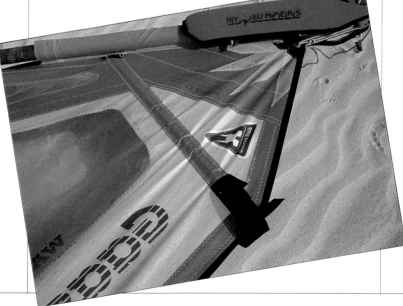

▶ *CARRYING YOUR EQUIPMENT*

Once assembled, board and rig should be carried separately. Depending on construction, the board alone may weigh anything up to 25 kilos, a fair weight to transport single-handed. If carried properly, the physical effort of getting the equipment to the water can be much reduced.

Prior to lifting, position the board onto its rail with the deck towards you.

In comparison with the board, provided the wind is light, the rig is easy to carry. Before lifting always position the rig so that the mast is directed into the wind with the clew pointing downwind. This will prevent you and the sail flipping over when the rig is picked up.

As the rig is lifted, the wind will funnel under it and

1 *Left* Stand near the balance-point of the board, between daggerboard and mast-socket, then take the main weight with one arm, using your fingers hooked through the daggerboard case. Use the fingers of the other hand in the mast-socket to maintain control and balance. Providing you are not already struggling it should be a relatively simple task to walk around with the board. If you are of slight build, you must look for an alternative method. The best solution may be to get someone else to help you — one of you at each end of the board.

2 *Below left* Raise one end of the board and move off whilst trailing the board behind you on the ground. Sand and shingle being abrasive, this practice will of course do little for the appearance of your board!

3 *Above* Approaching the rig to windward, place one hand on the mast above the boom and the other on the boom. Maintaining a firm grip, elevate the rig to waist height. This allows freedom for leg movement.

float it, making it feel lighter. If the beach is crowded, it may be necessary to lift the rig higher to avoid disturbing other beach users. Raising the front of the boom, get under the luff area of the sail and, face the direction in which you want to travel. If you find the wind blowing you around too much, revert to carrying the rig in the lower stance.

▶ *LAUNCHING*

If you stand on a beach watching sailboards being launched, you'll see that rarely are two identical methods used. The tried and trusted method is very simple and involves taking the two assembled parts (rig and board) and carrying them into the water separately. This is perfectly practical provided that the water is shallow with no surf or currents. Always carry the rig in first (up to knee-depth) as the rig is less likely to float away than the board. Return for the board and connect the two together. The majority of fittings require the board to be on its rail to attach the rig — so don't venture out too deep or your task will become increasingly difficult.

If you feel sufficiently confident, it is less time-consuming to launch the board with the rig already firmly in place. The complete assembly can be dragged into the water.

Proceed into the water to a sufficient depth for the fin and daggerboard to be completely clear of the bottom. Now you're ready for the real windsurfing.

▶ GETTING ON BOARD

Once you're ready to go you should be prepared for the first of numerous falls, so check that there is enough water-depth to make sure that you don't hit the bottom when your balance fails. Work out roughly the direction of the wind and align the board at 90° to its prevailing direction. The sail should lie downwind of the board, with the clew pointing towards the tail. The mast should be roughly perpendicular to the board.

Approach the board from the windward side, which should be opposite to the rig. Place both hands over the centreline (an imaginary line running directly between the nose and tail of the board).

1 *Above right* Support the rig completely above the head, stabilizing it with hands on boom and mast. A little wind will again relieve a proportion of the rig-weight.

2 With the board on its rail (to reduce friction and prevent the fin breaking) support the nose of the board under one arm. Standing to windward of the rig, take the front boom end with your other hand, and raise the rig clear of the ground.

1 *Top right* The front hand should be near the mast foot and the back hand a comfortable distance behind over the daggerboard. Pull yourself up over the board, keeping your weight over the centreline to maintain balance.

2 *Middle right* Move yourself into a kneeling position keeping the hands well-spaced and your weight still over the centreline. If you grasp the base of the uphaul, your position will be stabilized.

3 Firmly clasping the uphaul, move gently into a crouching position, with feet still on the centreline and placed one on each side of the mast foot, approximately shoulder width apart. Compose yourself in preparation for raising the rig — very important!

▶ *RAISING THE RIG*

Many sailors spend proportionately more time raising the rig — or uphauling — during their early days windsurfing than they will on any other manoeuvre in their entire sailing career. Although uphauling can be analyzed step by step, remember that in common with many moves in windsurfing it is not really sequential but flowing, and should be treated as such on the water.

Maintain a wide foot position while keeping the mast at right angles to the board.

1 *Above* Bend your knees, then with arms straight, begin to lean back slightly. The water will slowly but surely drain off from the top of the sail.

2 Using leg-pressure and body-weight pull the sail partially clear of the water. This process is liable to cause a bad back if performed incorrectly so keep the back as straight as possible to avoid unnecessary aches and pains.
As the sail lifts clear of the water it will begin to fill with wind and the board may start to move while the clew of the sail is still in the water. The board will stop when the sail is completely out of the water, so keep uphauling, pulling hand over hand.

3 Without the stabilizing effect of the rig in the water the board requires an extra degree of balance. To maintain this, keep your centre of gravity low by keeping the knees flexed.

4 *Below* From the head of the uphaul grasp the mast below the boom with the front hand or both hands, keeping arms extended. This secure position is comfortable and relaxed and should be returned to in any moments of uncertainty during subsequent sailing.
The wind is still blowing on your back. Your rig is at right angles to the board. Although the sail is flapping in the breeze, you will be stationary.

▶ *FEELING AT HOME*

The advantage gained from being familiar with your equipment is very much underestimated. In the earlier stages the sailor has little practical experience of board balance and rig-control. Rotating the board with the mast acting as an axis is good preparation for balancing on the moving object. The sailor will also get the feel of the reaction of the board resulting from his or her movement of the rig.

No two boards will act in exactly the same way in the water. The quicker the learner becomes familiar with his own rig and board, the better.

▶ *WINDWARD UPHAULING*

When you fall off, as you inevitably will, the rig will not always land in the best position for you to begin uphauling. Often the novice falls in backwards, and if he or she does not instantly let go of the rig it will land to windward of the board — the wrong side for conventional uphauling. Another uphauling technique must therefore be called into play in order that the rig be returned downwind, enabling the sailor to regain the secure position.

During windward uphauling the wind blows in your face instead of on your back.

1 *Above left* With a similar stance as before start to carefully lift the sail until it is partially clear of the water. Beware in strong airs as the wind is likely to get right underneath the sail and in a flash flick the sail violently onto the opposite side of the board, taking the sailor involuntarily with it!

2 *Left* When the sail is almost clear swing the rig (using the uphaul) towards the tail of the board, simultaneously balancing it with your body weight. You may find it easier to leave the rear boom end trailing in the water to prevent the rig swinging over too rapidly. Continue to pull the rig up and over the back of the board.

Shuffle your feet to a new position on the windward side as the rig comes round to the opposite side from where it started.

3 *Above* With the rig almost in the conventional uphauling position, the wind will be directed once again onto your back. When the mast is at right angles to the board uphauling can be resumed.
If you can prevent the sail touching the water as it crosses over onto the other side of the board, the time and effort will be saved and you can assume the secure position immediately.

1 *Left* Starting from the by now familiar secure position, incline the rig towards the back of the board. This can be done with your hands on the mast or at the head of the uphaul, whichever seems most comfortable.
The front of the board will turn into the wind. The rate at which it turns is directly correlated to the degree at which the rig is inclined — a steep inclination results in a rapid turn.

2 *Above left* As the board begins to turn, shuffle around the front of the board keeping feet close to the mast foot.
Take only small steps, as any dramatic movement will upset the balance of the board.

3 *Above* Still grasping the mast, continue to incline the rig in the same direction until the board has travelled through a complete 180° turn.
At this point tilt the mast forward until the board ceases turning any further.

4 *Left* Relocate your feet firmly over the centreline of the board and resume a new secure position.
The final result is that the board has turned 180° to face the opposite direction. Meanwhile the rig remains virtually in the same position in relation to the wind throughout. This is a useful manoeuvre to practice and one which greatly increases your confidence and competence in handling the board.

► *SAILING AWAY*

Even with only a limited amount of experience under your belt, sailing forward should be well within your capability. The simplest and easiest point of sailing to try first is a beam reach (sailing straight across the wind).

Looking from the secure position, establish a fixed goal roughly straight ahead. Before proceeding further make sure there are no obstacles in your path. Be sure to look around for other water users as with only minimal control of the board it will be difficult for you to avoid a collision.

1 *Left* Once the way is completely clear, release a hand from the secure position, and grasp the mast with the front hand only.

2 *Opposite below* Move the rear foot backwards over the daggerboard casing, but keep it placed on the board's centre line. The front foot should be placed behind the mast near the centre line, but facing towards the nose of the board. Keep the rig at right angles to the board by using the front hand. This is the start position.

As yet you have not moved anywhere. You must now execute a series of flowing movements to achieve the sailing position. Turn to face your goal and pull the rig to a balance point which should be near to your leading shoulder.

3 *Right* At the balance point the rig should feel weightless and you will probably find that the view downwind is obstructed by the sail. Rest your rear hand on the boom, and if you feel comfortable change your front hand from the mast to its appropriate place on the boom. Your hands should be about a shoulder-width apart on the boom.

4 *Below* Sheet in gradually with the back hand. The board will will begin to move. Now transfer your weight to the back foot in order to counteract the pull of the sail. The board will now be in a moving "sailing" position.

Lowering the rig. From the secure position, the front hand can be lowered down the mast and the rig in turn gently lowered into the water. The board should now be at a complete standstill.

Actually getting going will normally take a few attempts so to avoid numerous duckings, first practice it on dry land. When moving, the power generated in the rig must be balanced by leaning out your body-weight. Generally speaking, the stronger the wind the more the sailor has to lean. The rig power can be released by easing out the back hand and increased by pulling in. As the power increases do not forget to transfer more weight to the back foot.

Your initial sailing distances are likely to be fairly short. However, once you can sail for long distances the next thing you should know is how to stop in a controlled manner! Stopping is merely a process of reversing the sailing stages to revert back to the secure position.

▶ STEERING

If you watch somebody windsurfing, you'll see that it's very rarely that they sail in a straight line for any distance. In normal conditions all sailors need to alter their course while still heading in roughly the same direction. The reason for the change of course may be to avoid a buoy or other object in the water, or even a

1 *Above left* Steering into the wind. Assume the sailing position on a beam reach. The sail will lie at approximately 45° to the board.
Identify new goal that lies further upwind of the old one. Do not pick a goal too far upwind as it may be too much to attain in a single beat and therefore require upwind tacking in order to reach it.

2 *Above right* Draw the rig across the body and towards the back of the board. This is all one movement facilitated by extending the back arm. The main movement here is undertaken primarily by arms and shoulders.
The immediate result is that the nose of the board will begin to turn towards the wind. As the board points towards the new goal, tilt the rig forward and return to a normal sailing position.

3 *Left* You are now on a point of sailing closer to the wind. To maintain power the rig must be sheeted in with the back hand. Take care not to point too much into the wind or you will lose both momentum and control.

similar craft sailing on a collision course from the opposite direction. In either case, you have to avoid a collision. The simple answer is just to stop, but a better solution is to steer round the obstruction. In the later stages of your sailing career, changes in heading may be more subtle; for example, responding to wind shifts when racing. Changing course in these circumstances may not be absolutely imperative but is nevertheless a good tactic.

▶ STEERING INTO THE WIND

When practising steering initially, it is a good idea to do it out of the way of other water users until your competence has increased. Ideally the wind should be light (below 10 knots) because then you will be punished less for any mistakes you may make. A brief recap on the theory — as you tilt the mast aft, the force upon the sail (centre of effort) will move back in relation to the daggerboard (centre of resistance). The board will pivot towards the wind.

▶ STEERING AWAY FROM THE WIND

Pointing higher upwind is only half of the story. For all-round sailing ability you must be able to steer off the newly found close-hauled course and return to your original heading. In effect, you will have sailed a zig-zag course. The technique of sailing away from the wind is called bearing off (or bearing away) and requires a higher degree of control than the heading up manoeuvre. It is a good exercise — and also fun — to alternate heading up and bearing away movements in quick succession. This produces an exhilarating feeling of control.

Assume the close-hauled position as just described (sailing into the wind).

1 *Top right* Steering away from the wind. Draw the rig across the body and incline the mast to windward, extending the front arm and sheeting in with the back hand. Be careful at this point not to get overpowered as you are effectively presenting more sail-area to the wind. There is a risk of getting pulled over the front of the board. The centre of effort in the sail will move forward of the daggerboard (resistance) allowing the front of the board to pivot away from the wind.

2 *Middle right* When the board is pointing to the original goal tilt the rig backwards to cease bearing away any further. Now return to the normal sailing position.

3 The new course is now broad relative to the wind so ease out the back hand slightly to re-establish comfort and power.

▼ Typically the novice adopts a frog-like sailing stance with arms and legs too far apart. It is aesthetically more pleasing and more comfortable for the legs and arms to be at similar distances (shoulder width apart).

▶ *STANCE*

Incorrect sailing stance may not *initially* inhibit your performance a great deal, but the chances are that it will lead to problems in the long run.

When sailing with the correct stance one feels relaxed and comfortable. The back should be straight, arms slightly bent and knees flexed. The object of the exercise is to let the wind do the work — your body should be transmitting these forces to the board with the minimum of effort.

A common mistake which will be familiar to anyone who has either watched or instructed beginners is that of sticking out the backside. This is a perfectly understandable reaction to instability, but makes control almost impossible to achieve because the body weight is wrongly distributed on the board.

When sailing, keep your body weight over the centre line in order to keep the board level. If you are too far away from the centreline the board will rail up and you will be tipped into the water.

▼ The correct sailing stance.

► UPWIND AND TACKING

Having mastered the art of sailing in a straight line without falling off, you'll soon need to know how to turn round and come back. The method of turning most readily learned is *tacking*, which involves turning the nose of the board through the wind.

Unfortunately many beginners seem to develop a psychological blockage regarding this manoeuvre. For them the tack is synonymous with taking a dip at the end of every reach! In reality it is *not* as difficult as it seems, and skill and confidence can rapidly be gained with practice. If the manoeuvres are rehearsed in relatively calm conditions, where keeping one's balance is not complicated by waves or a swell on the water, there is no reason why rapid progress should not be made.

Tacking really comes into play when the sailor decides that he/she wants to change course and head towards a new goal point which is directly upwind. Sailing theory, however, only allows upwind progression within a defined area. A line (about 45° upwind) delineates an area known as the no-go zone which marks the limit of your upwind ability. A goal within this area is impossible to achieve on a single point of sailing.

The sailor must therefore execute a complete change of direction onto a close-haul on the opposite tack, the aim being to zig-zag upwind in the direction of the desired goal. With this change in direction the sailor must tack the board to arrive on the new course. If the goal is some distance upwind, it is advisable to put in a number of small tacks.

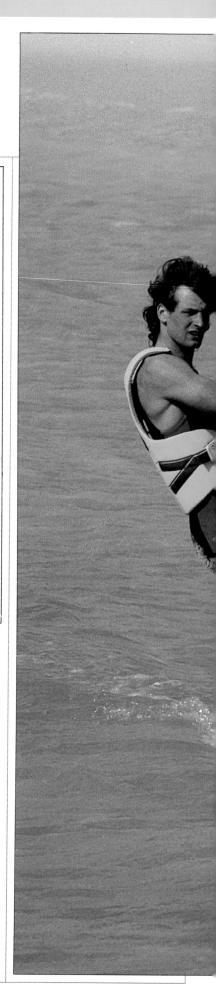

TACKING TO WINDWARD

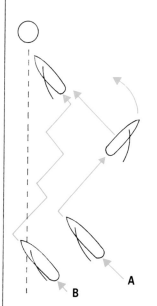

The goal in this instance can be achieved with one tack by following the path of board A. If the wind changes direction a little you may find that you are in fact losing ground away from the goal. If the path of board B is followed, the chances of this occurring are reduced.

1 Close hauled: Steer the board onto a new course, as close to the wind as possible.

2 *Far right* Steer the board gradually into the wind. Simultaneously move your front foot in front of (but adjacent to) the mast foot.
It is important to be aware of the sail position. Take care not to get trapped by the sail as the board turns into the wind. If you have not already moved your feet forward it will be impossible to stand on the forward part of the board. Keep on inclining the rig towards the back of the board to continue the turn.

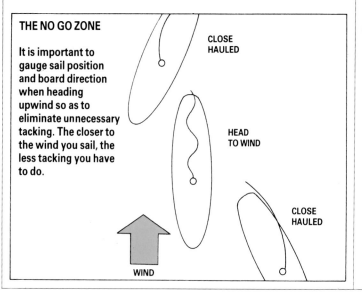

THE NO GO ZONE

It is important to gauge sail position and board direction when heading upwind so as to eliminate unnecessary tacking. The closer to the wind you sail, the less tacking you have to do.

CLOSE HAULED

HEAD TO WIND

CLOSE HAULED

WIND

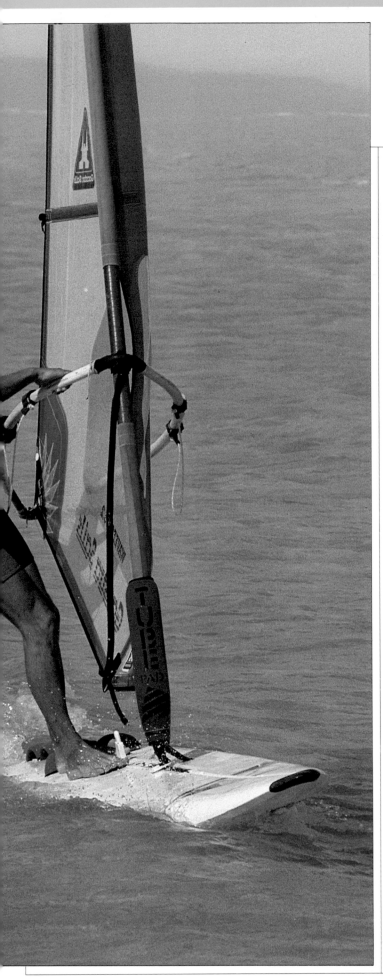

A point exists when it is no longer feasible to sail any closer-hauled to the wind. There is a very narrow margin of error and attempting to point too high will result in the board heading directly into wind and stopping. Pointing too low will result in inefficient sailing as a large number of tacks will be necessary in order to achieve the goal.

To attain the optimum heading when close-hauled, steer further into the wind until the luff area of the sail begins to back-wind. As it does so you will start to slow down. You are obviously too close to the wind and should consequently bear away just a little until more power returns to the sail. When you decide to initiate the tack, transfer your front hand from the boom onto the mast.

3 *Right* Shuffle your other foot in front of the mast, transferring your back hand to meet your front hand on the mast at the same time. Shuffle completely around the mast as the board turns around onto the new tack.

4 *Middle right* With hands still in place, but now on the opposite tack, take up the secure position before moving off.
You have now successfully completed your first tack. The rest come easier!

▶ DOWNWIND AND GYBING

Gybing is the second method of turning the board through 180° onto an opposite tack. The principle involved is simple. Whereas in tacking the board is turned *upwind*, in gybing the board is turned *downwind*. Before attempting to execute a gybe the sailor should understand the theory of downwind sailing.

As is the case with many windsurfing manoeuvres, dry-land practice is recommended to gain the rudimentary principles of rig control. Rig control is critical when sailing downwind. While sailing on a reach it is easy to use the rig as a counter-balance but as you bear further downwind it becomes increasingly difficult to do this.

Your first attempt at a gybe is likely to be extremely precarious and tentative. Repeated practice is the only way to boost confidence. With expert guidance the learning process will be considerably shorter and easier. Light winds provide the ideal conditions for learning, preferably winds of less than 10 knots. Once again, flat water is essential.

The gybe involves the easily grasped concept of flipping the rig. Be sure you have ample room to execute the manoeuvre and check downwind for other water-users.

1 *Bottom right* To initiate the gybe from a normal sailing position across the wind first draw the rig across your body. Incline the mast both forward and to windward by extending your front arm (a similar process to steering away from the wind). The front of the board will turn away from the wind. Continue the rig motion across the body, easing the power off a little with the back hand. The board will continue to turn, but at a slower rate.
You should now be thinking about flipping the sail. Transfer your back hand directly *under* your front hand and onto the mast.

2 *Far right* Move your front foot back so that it is parallel to your rear foot. Position both feet either side of the centre line, facing forward. The board will balance if equal weight is applied to each foot.
The sail is at 90° to the board and you are briefly on a new point of sailing known as the *run*.
To maintain control on the run, angle the rig towards you a little. This will effectively reduce the sail area presented to the wind. Keep your centre of gravity low and your weight back to avoid being lifted from the deck.

▶ *IMPROVER'S TACK*

This hybrid tack is a direct extension of the afore-mentioned beginner's tack. The improver's tack is particularly useful in moderate breezes when its superior speed becomes really apparent. In even stronger winds the rig power can be used to much better effect, especially when inclining the rig to initiate the turn.

The rapid change from tack to tack is useful when the water-surface is choppy. Wind-blown chop is renowned for upsetting the sailor's equilibrium when part-way through the tack, therefore this tack is useful as, when mastered, progressively less time is spent with no wind in the sail. The board is therefore continually powered through the turn and less at the mercy of the water movement. There is also a side-effect worth mentioning; in the basic tack the sailor has a long period with no sail power, and therefore has to rely solely on distribution of body-weight to balance the board. During the improved tack this balancing-time is much reduced. If a sailor has any aspirations to race in his or her later career then this quicker tack is a most useful trick to learn.

Ideal conditions for practice are a steady force three to four wind and flat water, although in this

3 *Right* The sail will now begin to swing around the nose of the board through wind pressure alone.

As it starts to swing, you must release your front hand from the boom to avoid being helicoptered around with the rig. As the rig swings, be careful not to catch the clew in the water as this will upset your balance. (If you have an old-style sail with a characteristically long boom which is inclined to catch the water very easily, you must try to keep the rig more vertical throughout this process.)

Before moving off on the new tack, either attain a secure position or go straight to the start position. Once you can repeatedly pull off a successful gybe concentrate on making the movements flow smoothly so that the gybe appears as one continuous process.

1 *Left* Improver's tack. The rig is sheeted in and inclined to such an extent that the clew almost touches the water. With full weight committed to your back foot the board will swing quickly towards the wind. Lateral back foot pressure will increase the rate at which the board swings.

2 *Above* right To avoid being trapped place your front foot just in front of the mast-foot. Position your front hand onto the mast. Now commit your body-weight forward in preparation for moving round in front of the mast.

The nose of the board will have travelled completely through the eye of the wind.

3 *Left* Quickly make a break for the front section of the board. It is important not to release your rear hand from the boom until you have started to move forward as the mast will fall to leeward into an irretrievable position. Be wary of releasing the rear hand too early — a common (and often disastrous) mistake. As you step round the front of the board, transfer the mast from one hand to the other. Foot movements should be swift since the board at this point will be almost on its new tack. Keep foot movements to a minimum — a few positive steps about the centre line will not disrupt the board's balance unduly. Some sailors advocate jumping around the mast but if badly executed this will only disturb your equilibrium.

4 *Right* All that now remains is to sheet in with the back hand. Your front can now be repositioned onto the boom. This process should be done as quickly as possible in order to maintain speed and regain balance.

1 *Middle* Flare gybing. Try to keep your body-weight forward while moving your feet further back on the board. At the same time move your hands along the boom towards the rear end. Maintain pressure on the windward rail otherwise the board will luff back onto its original heading.

2 *Top right* Increase the pressure on the windward rail with your front foot. The board will begin to turn sharply. Pressure should be kept on the leeward rail with the back foot to prevent the board from literally turning over. The rig is inclined back to prevent overpowering. For maximum turning pressure, the rig is inclined steeply to windward.

3 *Bottom right* As the board passes through the run position, the power in the sail will automatically decrease. Incline the rig further to windward, still maintaining your weight over the centreline and keeping your knees flexed to maintain balance.
The tail of the board may be completely submerged so keep a little weight through the mast-foot in anticipation of refloating the tail.
With the nose being completely clear of the water the board will pivot instantly onto its new tack. As the board approaches the new tack move forward while still maintaining slight pressure on the old windward rail until the board is completely around.

breeze you'll probably find slight wind-blown chop. Assume the normal sailing position on a beam reach. Due to the wind strength your board may just be planing. The initial turn towards the wind must be fairly sharp, so with both hands still on the boom, incline the rig back steeply, while at the same time sheeting in hard with the back hand.

When you are safely sailing on the opposite tack settle down into the correct sailing position. The secret of the improver's tack is timing. First practise the moves at a slower pace, when your sense of timing is more developed you may attempt progressively quicker turns. You will soon find that basic tacking is transformed into a new dynamic form.

▶ FLARE GYBING

Prior to the now common short board carve gybe, the flare gybe was the most effective way of turning the board through 180°. For triangle racers today it is still an essential manoeuvre when rounding downwind marks.

Rig control during the flare gybe is in some respects similar to the basic gybe. The speed of the turn is governed largely by board movement. Obviously it takes a while to develop the necessary board skills, but once mastered this gybe is one of the most exhilarating ways of turning a long board.

The main advantages of the flare gybe are twofold. Firstly, the gybe is a quick transition from tack to tack and secondly, the board is turned in such a small area that very little ground is lost downwind. The ideal wind for initial attempts is a force two. However, the flare gybe can be used to good effect in much stronger airs that demand a higher degree of balance

and rig-control.

Maintain a sailing position roughly across the wind. Make sure that the daggerboard is *down* as this will give an extra degree of turn and increased stability. The tightness of the turn is directly related to the amount of daggerboard protruding. Search for a flat section of water in which to turn, checking for plenty of room downwind.

Bear away onto a broad reach bending your knees slightly — you will need to do this to counteract the influence of the daggerboard.

When you have managed a few successful gybes, concentrate on making the movement smooth and flowing. As your sense of timing becomes more acute, you will find it possible to move further back on the board up to a point when the board will pivot within its own length.

1 *Left* Positioning the board for a beach start. Keep the sail powered with the back hand, and pull the front of the board towards you by raising the front hand.
Maintain a firm stance and draw the front of the board through an arc between yourself and the mast foot.

2 *Below left* As the board passes through the eye of the wind release your rear hand. The sail will then flip over.

4 *Above* Completing the gybe. You are now on a new tack, but the sail is pointing clew-first. Place your nearest hand adjacent to the front boom end. Using it as a pivot let the rig flip around the nose of the board.

5 *Left* As your skill develops you'll be able to turn the board very sharply.

▶ BEACH STARTING

Beach starting is often associated exclusively with short-board sailing as the high-wind sailor is frequently seen performing this manoeuvre in breaking surf and high wind. In these circumstances uphauling is out of the question. But beach starting is also very useful to the beginner who faces with trepidation the prospect of having to uphaul the rig each time he or she wants to get under way. Instead of constantly fighting against the wind to pull the sail up, it is possible — and a good deal more elegant — to let the wind do most of the work and pull you on to the board.

Ideally this manoeuvre should be attempted in shallow launching areas, preferably where there is hard sand underfoot. If the bottom shelves too quickly you may be out of your depth before you realize it.

For initial practice the wind should be nearly cross-shore, blowing about a Force 2.

Before you can *really* enjoy sailing you must first be able to achieve a clean start. What often happens in reality is that having got the board pointing across the wind and out to sea, by the time you have decided to heave yourself aboard the wind has moved into another position.

Therefore it is extremely useful to be able to beach start, i.e. jump onto the board in the shallows with the rig already raised. The key to success is to keep the rig clear of the water and let the wind do all the work. You'll save energy as you won't have to abandon the rig to wrestle the board into position.

To make the board easier to handle, retract the daggerboard as far as possible. Any pressure directed through the mast-foot will now make the board pivot about the skeg, and therefore be more manageable.

▶ POSITIONING THE BOARD

From an awkward position with the board facing the shoreline, practice manoeuvring the board into a position suitable for beach-starting. For this exercise the wind should be blowing at right angles to the board. To gain maximum leverage on the board, hold the mast above the boom with the front hand. Hold the boom itself with the back hand only at the rig's balance point.

Beach starting technique is also useful to the advanced sailor. It can be readily applied to short boards in high wind and surf situations.

▶ GETTING ONTO THE BOARD

When you feel confident of achieving the starting position (after positioning the board) push the board onto a broad reach.

It is easy to realize the advantages of the beach start. The sailor arrives on his/her board and moves forward in one smooth movement. Above all else he/she is completely dry.

3 *Far left* Replace both hands onto the boom and push the board away using pressure through the mast foot. The board should now be on a beam reach, the correct position.

4 *Below left* Bring the board adjacent to your body then lift your back foot onto the centre line of the board.
Maintain the board's broad reach heading with pressure through the mast foot. You can control the considerable pull in the sail with the back hand, as when sailing.

5 *Above left* To gain lift, straighten both arms vertically. This will present more effective sail area to the wind and so maximize potential lift.
Combine a little hop with your front foot to facilitate extra lift which will pull you out of the water. If you time this to coincide with a small gust the task will be made simpler. *Do not* use the boom as a bar to pull against otherwise you will fall flat on your back into the water. You must only use enough power to counteract the pull of the sail.
Once you are completely aboard, power the sail instantly with the rear hand and bear away slightly to prevent the board luffing into wind.

6 *Left* You can immediately assume a sailing position.

▶ THE BOARD

The term 'board' is often used loosely and generally refers to the package of hull, footstraps, daggerboard and mastfoot. The hull is commonly constructed from ABS plastic or polyethylene, the former being cheaper to produce and more hard-wearing. Polyethylene has in the past had something of a bad name for its quality of finish, but this is not true of today's polyethylene boards. Slightly more up-market boards tend to be made from ABS or even fibreglass. Fibreglass is particularly strong and naturally stiff. The resulting boards are lightweight and if they are of good design, very competitive. The fibreglass boards whether polyester or epoxy, do not withstand everyday knocks quite as well as plastic constructions; therefore they need to be treated with care.

The most important aspect of the board performance-wise is its hydrodynamics, or underwater shape. Modern boards all incorporate a slight vee in the tail section. This vee aids directional stability and allows rail-to-rail pivoting during turns. More complex underwater profiles do exist and are used mainly on funboards. These profiles revolve around concave configurations. The aim is to promote lift and consequently early planing. The board's rail shape can also affect its planing point—and its upwind ability. Square type rails facilitate good upwind performance, whilst rounder rails give better grip. The solution is usually a compromise between the two.

The tandem is steered in the same manner as a conventional board, but is generally slower to react.

The concept of the multi-rig board is here taken to the extreme. Sailing in these circumstances becomes a social event, with considerable spectator appeal!

Although the camber-induced rig is fast in fast conditions, it is not suitable for the beginner. When in the water, the large luff sleeve fills with water, making the rig heavy. When uphauling, the fixed-profile sail does tend to cradle water and hamper proceedings.

▶ *TANDEMS*

A board which you will not often see is the tandem board which incorporates two rigs. Tandems require a lot of skill and co-ordination from the two sailors. As can be imagined, tacking and gybing — which can be tricky enough on a solo board — are particularly difficult in tandem.

Despite their disadvantages, tandems are a lot of fun to sail and when used with just one rig, can double as a useful teaching apparatus.

▶ *SAILS*

Sail design has certainly come a long way since the early days of windsurfing. Over the last couple of years sails have finally become relatively stable to use. Design change has been mainly cosmetic, however, and we have moved more towards a concept of sail design for specific purposes. The sail *you* choose should be suitable for the type of sailing you intend taking up.

Sails are constructed from many types of cloth for which there are a variety of different trade-names. Basically cloths are either *Dacron* or *Mylar* composites. Dacron, the cheaper of the two, tends to be used for sails at the lower priced end of the board market. The main drawback of this material is that it will stretch with extended use and eventually lose its shape, becoming increasingly difficult to set. The more expensive mylar does not stretch and is commonly used for high-performance rigs. The mylar itself is merely a plastic-type film laminated on to one side of the sailcloth. With time, some mylars may start to delaminate. This process can be accelerated by exposure to strong sunlight. Scrim and tri-laminate variations of mylar are an attempt to increase the sail's strength and anti-rip characteristics. With such a mylar, a small rip will not develop rapidly into a large tear. Water will drain off the laminate quickly, and the saving in rig-weight can be felt by even the basic sailor.

The beginner has benefited immensely from the rapid pace of sail development. There are basically two forms of sail available. These are termed *hard-set sails* (fixed profiles) and *softer set sails*. The extreme hard sail is the *camber-induced rig*. The camber in this sail is induced by plastic tuning forks in the leading edge. The number of tuning forks (camber inducers) may vary from model to model. The main function of efficiency is maintained in all wind-

strengths, as the camber encourages really smooth air-flow on the leeward side of the sail.

The *rotational* sail is another fixed profile sail incorporating full-length battens. Its principle of efficiency is again to do with smooth air-flow over the leeward side of the sail. To achieve this, the battens rest against the mast. During manoeuvres the battens will flip to the other side of the mast as you arrive on a new tack. The rotational is a good all-round sail and quite easy to handle as its centre of effort moves only marginally.

The *cutaway* sail is the most recent development from the world's top sail lofts. The concept of the cutaway is quite simple: when overpowered, the head will fall away and spill wind from the leech area so making for easier control. After a gust, the head will fall back to regain correct amount of power. The handling is not altered throughout wind-changes.

A cutaway sail with full length battens is again not the ideal thing to use in the early stages of sailing. The rotational and cutaway can be used to greatest effect once the basic manoeuvres are mastered.

A soft-set sail is the type best suited to the beginner as the luff area can be used as a guide to trim and wind-direction. There are very few exclusively soft sails to choose from, more often the rotational/cutaway sail incorporates a dual batten system. This allows the sail's middle full length battens to be substituted by half-battens to achieve a soft setting luff area. Once a sailor's proficiency increases the full length battens can be introduced if required.

The most important things that a beginner should look for when choosing a rig are a boom of reasonable length, a strong mast and a sail that is not going to be difficult to uphaul.

▶ SAIL CARE

Sails of decent quality have never come cheap and today is no exception. It is therefore sensible to look after your equipment. If you stick to a few simple rules, the life of your sail can be greatly extended.

● Do not rig up on stony ground or in car-parks as this will definitely have a detrimental effect — especially on mylar sails. Doing so can result in scratches, abrasions and even tears. When on the shoreline avoid placing the rig in the vicinity of any sharp objects. Remember that even in a slight breeze the wind can flip the sail over, possibly onto a sharp object capable of puncturing it.

● Tar deposits are a great bugbear for windsurfers. The sail will readily pick up tar or oil if it is left lying on the beach. If a stain does appear, you should remove it at the first opportunity. Do not use any powerful solvents to remove these substances as they may break down the structure of the sailcloth. It is a good idea simply to use washing-up liquid and warm water which generally does the trick.

● When de-rigging, always release the downhaul first. If the outhaul is released first the luff of the sail will be excessively loaded and could possibly be pulled out of shape.

1 *Above* The rotational sail is an ideal intermediate sail, but again is not suited to the absolute beginner for the same reasons as the camber inducer.

2 *Far right* The cutaway sail has recently given rise to much controversy, particularly concerning its high-wind performance.

3 *Right* It only takes a matter of a few minutes to change over the battens used on a dual batten system sail.

4 *Top right* Storing the sail. The sail should be rolled from head to foot in order to prevent creases. Again, this is particularly important with mylar sails as they tend to crack easily if folded.

● When you have finished sailing, do not release the outhaul and permit the sail to flap around in the breeze. Although this will dry it off nicely, it will fatigue the sailcloth and possibly cause delamination.

● To further prolong sail-life you should rinse the sail until it is free of salt water after every session. This is not always convenient, but do remember that salt water over time will attack the stitching that holds the sail together.

● The rolled sail should always be kept in a sail bag.

► *WETSUITS*

Unless you have the good fortune to live in a climate that is hot all the year round a wetsuit is going to be an absolute necessity. Wetsuits also enable the sailor in temperate climates to make maximum use of his/her board. The function of a wetsuit is to keep the body at a comfortable temperature whilst sailing. In

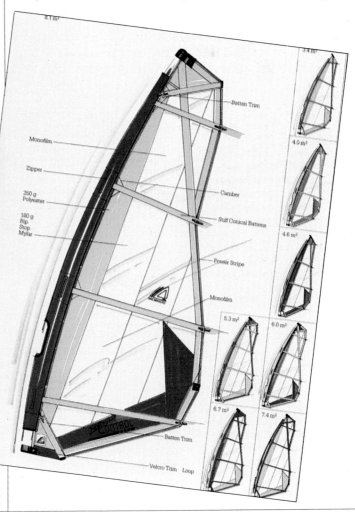

order to work properly, the wetsuit has to be a close fit in order that such water as does get in is trapped within the suit and heated up by your body temperature.

Wetsuits are generally made of neoprene covered by nylon on one or both sides. To give them comfort and ease of entry the inside is always lined. The outside of the suit is often left with no lining as it will be warmer — water will run straight off — and thus the cooling effect of wind-chill and evaporation is reduced. This single-lined type of suit is however more susceptible to snagging and tearing. For the novice who spends much time scrambling onto the board a suit with lining on the outside (double-lined) is much more hard-wearing.

Wetsuits use one of three main types of stitching, overlocking, Mauser-tape, and blind-stitch.

These are the traditional methods of stitching. However, recently some manufacturers have been hot-air heat sealing their seams (sealing a tape across the inside of the already glued seam) and claim that this method is also strong and totally waterproof.

Often it is still necessary to wear a wet-suit of some description in warm climates. Prolonged exposure to warm wind will cause a chilling effect. The minimum wet-suit coverage is usually in the form of a vest — often used by sailors in Hawaii. As the wind increases the chill factor becomes more apparent and a suit with more body-coverage is required. The style of suit to fit the bill depends on the water and air temperature prevailing at the time.

If the sailor feels cold on the water, summer suits may be supplemented by additional garments. The classic long-john usually has a corresponding bolero top, the sleeves of which can either be neoprene or nylon. More recently some short-arm steamers have been manufactured with detachable arms, making the suit useful over a wider temperature-range.

If you sail in cold climates during the winter your choice of suit is restricted to a winter steamer (a thick, sealed wetsuit) or a dry-suit, both of which offer excellent protection against the elements. The winter steamer is usually made from 4 or 5 mm neoprene. This thicker neoprene retains more heat than the thinner variety, and lends itself well to the blind-stitching technique. In order to work efficiently a winter-suit must be a good fit as this will help to reduce water-penetration to a minimum.

TYPES OF STITCHING

Overlocking is the simplest method of construction, but water-penetration of the suit is quite high due to the fact that the seams are not glued prior to stitching. A suit made by this method is really only appropriate for warmer conditions. A mauser-tape construction, although glued and incorporating tape over the seam, still allows relatively high water-penetration. This process is commonly used in the making of two-piece suits, i.e. the long-john and bolero. The most watertight of all the construction methods is the blind-stitch suit. Prior to stitching the suit is glued along all seams. When stitching the needle does not pass through the neoprene but only pierces the surface to a depth of approximately two millimetres. This method can only be practically employed on neoprene thicker than 3 mm. The warmest suits for extreme conditions are blind-stitched as water-penetration is minimized by using this method.

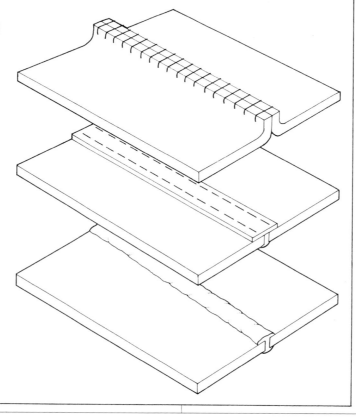

1 *Top right* In warm, windy conditions, the sailor should wear either a long john or a variation on the summer steamer. The variations can take many forms either having short arms, short legs or both.

2 *Middle right* When buying a winter suit, it is sometimes difficult to choose between the steamer and the dry-suit. The steamers in general work out much cheaper — and this may be the decisive factor that accounts for their popularity. Dry suits are, it must be said, prone to damage, especially in the seal-areas. A damaged neck-seal is very dangerous as the suit can quickly fill with water, sinking its wearer without trace!

3 Cold weather accessories.

Dry suits work according to a different principle. As the name suggests, they aim to keep the wearer completely dry. In order to do this they incorporate seals around the neck, wrists and ankles. If maintained properly, these will keep the water out. The dry suit can fit either closely or loosely — the former style is a much more practical proposition. If it is extremely cold, thin clothing may be worn underneath.

There are a variety of other accessories that can be used in particularly cold weather to complement the winter suit. When temperature drops, sailors usually reach first for a pair of wet-suit boots. Ideally, these should be blind-stitched. The hands are also very prone to cold, making it necessary to wear wetsuit gloves — although if these are too bulky they will hamper the sailor's feel for the rig. Hands are especially susceptible to wind-chill, whether gloves are worn or not.

The greatest source of heat-loss is the unprotected head. Sometimes as much as 30 per cent of body-heat may be lost in this manner. In severe cold it is most advisable to use either a hat or a hood. The latter is preferable in that it covers the back of the neck.
A wind-top has slightly wider scope for use. It will reduce wind-chill if worn on top of a winter suit, but is also useful as a substitute for a bolero in warmer conditions.

▶ HARNESSES

The *harness* is basically a buoyancy-aid which incorporates a hook at the front. This hook is used in conjunction with *harness-lines*, short pieces of covered rope attached to the boom. Their function is to relieve strain on the sailor's arms when the sailor's harness lines are 'hooked-in' to the harness hook.

In general, harnesses are made from a core of closed celled foam (watertight) covered by nylon. Webbing is used to reinforce the harness and to locate the hook.

For the novice who spends a large proportion of his time in the water, the buoyancy aspect is of paramount importance. It must be realized, however, that harnesses are *not* life-jackets and that they will not support an unconscious sailor in the safe, "face-up" position. However some models *do* offer higher degrees of buoyancy than others. If you want a harness that will support your body-weight, test it by floating in the water. With both arms raised, your head should stay above the surface.

A good harness is generally comfortable to wear.

With continuous use it should not cause stress, but should support the susceptible lower-back region. If the harness is a bad fit it will not give proper support and will also tend to ride up during use. Harnesses do come in various sizes, so try before you buy — and remember that a good model should be adjustable.

There is really only one type of acceptable hook, so check that your proposed purchase has the vee-shaped hook that is "tangle-free". Be particularly wary of the single-pronged hook around which the rope can get entangled or trapped too easily. This is potentially hazardous should you fall in still attached to the lines and with the sail on top of you. Your harness should incorporate a quick-release buckle enabling a speedy escape in any difficult situation.

Often the hook is combined with a spreader-bar arrangement. This bar spreads the body-weight over the ribs instead of concentrating it at one single point. It also makes sailing more comfortable.

Safety apart, many teaching establishments insist on the use of personal buoyancy aids. Waist and seat harnesses may not satisfy these requirements. Do remember that quality harnesses are not cheap. They will, however, last longer and give better service and therefore prove to be the sounder investment.

▶ MASTS

The mast (or spar) is a vital part of the rigging. Although it obviously supports the sail, it also affects the sail's set.

Masts vary in stiffness but most sails will set reasonably on any mast. If vertical creases appear in the luff area this is a sign that the mast is not stiff enough. A stiffer spar must be substituted in order to improve the sail-set. However if you're windsurfing on a tight budget then the bendy mast will suffice.

A couple of years ago masts were available in different base diameters, the more common ones being 46 mm/1⅘ in and 48.5 mm/1⁹⁄₁₀ in. The latter diameter has now become almost standard. Masts are manufactured from fibreglass (epoxy) or aluminium. The epoxy mast is much stronger and consequently more versatile for different styles of sailing, be this on the local pond or in mast-high waves. The main argument in favour of aluminium is its weight, saving perhaps two kilos over the epoxy mast. Such a saving may be critical to an international racer but is of little consequence to the novice. Some high-performance sails are cut for aluminium masts and will therefore not set well on epoxy ones.

Left A high-buoyancy harness is an asset in the early days of learning, especially if the sailor is not a proficient swimmer. It is possible to get flotation pads for the shoulder type of harness that fit inside the webbing on the front of the sailor.

Above The seat-harness offers the intermediate sailor better control and comfort for all-round sailing. It is, however, very low on buoyancy — in fact there is virtually no flotation for the upper part of the body. Using the seat-harness will give maximum leverage on the rig which explains why this version is so popular with high-speed sailors.

Below right The waist harness allows the greatest freedom of movement. It is therefore popular with more advanced funboard sailors, especially wave-riders. Buoyancy is again at a minimum.

Top right Shown here are the three different materials used in mast-manufacture.

Although they may appear strong, masts are breakable if undue strain is placed upon them. Be particularly careful of shore-breaks — and also of heavy vehicles in car parks! The epoxy mast is cheaper to replace in case of a mishap.

It is common to see carbon-fibre used in conjunction with epoxy in mast-manufacture. Carbon-fibre does little for overall strength, but does give stiffer bend characteristics.

An unusual concept — but one that works — is the pre-bent mast. The classic example is the Rotho Duo mast, the stiffness of which can be altered, depending on which side is used for the leading edge.

▶ BOOMS

Booms generally take two forms — either fixed or adjustable in length. The latter seems to be finding increasing favour with the windsurfing fraternity.

The adjustable booms of old have a reputation for being heavy and prone to break under pressure. More recent models are more reliable and weigh only slightly more than the fixed boom of similar length. The body of the boom is made of aluminium covered with a form of grip to protect the hands from contact with bare metal.

A good boom will generally incorporate soft grip which is kinder to the hands, reducing the abrasive effect of prolonged sailing. The boom ends are made from moulded plastic and take various forms, some more satisfactory than others.

The real test of a quality boom is its strength and stiffness. A boom should be able to withstand the rigour of time and the pressures imposed on it by rough conditions. To test a boom's stiffness it can be compressed by the sailor; if it flexes unduly, the handling characteristics of the rig will be adversely affected.

Sail profile is sometimes pre-determined by the front boom-end fitting. A wide (90°) front end would generally indicate compatibility with full profile sails. A narrower profile has more versatility and may be used with the majority of sails.

▶ MAST-TRACKS

There are only a few types of board-fittings to which the mast-foot is anchored. The traditional method is probably the most basic. This involves a mast-socket that is built into the board. The variation of mast-sockets depends upon the manufacturer of a particular model. In general older boards tend to have this type of fitting. The mast-foot is usually secured by a pin or by a locking mechanism within the mast-foot itself. Be sure that the method used by your particular board is reliable. There is nothing worse than sailing along in a leisurely manner and then have the mast-foot pop out. If your system has a habit of doing this, then use a safety leash. When the components separate, the leash will prevent them from drifting too far apart.

The sliding mast-track system is frequently incorporated on more up-to-date equipment. The track itself is either fitted directly onto the deck or recessed down a little to make the deck less cluttered. The track is usually operated by a foot lever which releases a temporary locking mechanism. The mast can then be repositioned whilst sailing.

The mast foot itself usually slots into a slider that runs along or within the track itself.

Modern booms adjust in various fashions and by differing lengths. A quality boom is generally easy to adjust. It should be kept in a clean, sand-free condition when not in use.

The sliding track is another product developed originally for the race course. Like so many good ideas it has recently been incorporated onto most new production boards. The advantages of being able to move the mast whilst sailing are apparent for racing and leisure sailors alike. When sailing upwind the mast should be positioned at the front of the track to increase waterline length, so the board points higher upwind. For downwind sailing the mast should be pulled back to achieve the reverse effect and give efficient planing off the wind.

If your board has a track system do not initially complicate things by trying to move it while afloat — master the basic manoeuvres first.

Many shorter boards, particularly custom boards have a fin-box recessed into the deck to act as the mast track. With a shorter board there is little need to move the mast once the correct position for the rider has been found. Special mast feet are available to fit the fin-box arrangement. The whole system is extremely strong. The box is fibreglassed firmly into the board and the mast foot spreads the rig's load over a large area. A single stringered custom board will often have a twin mast box assembly — this not only equalizes the load even more but gets round the problem of cutting into the stringer and weakening the overall structure of the board.

▼ A good track, if free of sand, should slide fore and aft with no problem. To aid movement the sailor should simultaneously pull or push the rig in the required direction. It is a good idea to wash out your mast-track frequently with fresh water to prevent it from sticking.

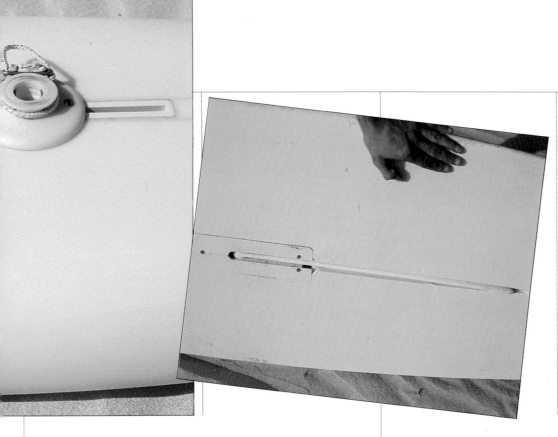

Far left The mast-track box. This is a common feature on custom boards. It allows the mast position to be adjusted when tuning for peak performance.

Left It is difficult to get a fully retracting system that incorporates the large daggerboard required for stability and for light-wind racing. The often small retracting dagger still offers ample stability for the novice as well as upwind performance in strong airs.

▶ *DAGGERBOARDS*

Where long boards are concerned, the daggerboard is almost as essential as the mast. A board will not perform well upwind unless it has a daggerboard in the *down* position.

Daggerboards are usually made from plastic even though this material does tend to flex — sometimes when going upwind this means that the balance of the board can be adversely affected. For serious racing, daggerboards made from wood or even aluminium are more satisfactory as these materials have better lateral stiffness.

Daggerboards work according to various different principles. In older models of board the daggerboard is generally fixed. For downwind sailing it was necessary to withdraw the daggerboard completely and sling it over the arm. The pivoting system introduced later can be operated with the feet. When beating, the daggerboard should be in the fully down position, and when reaching, the daggerboard can be pivoted up to prevent the board railing up at speed and tipping the rider off.

The ultimate compromise is perhaps the fully retracting system particularly common in today's race and funboards. To achieve maximum speed and downwind control the dagger can be positioned in such a way that it disappears completely into the hull where it can have no adverse effects on the board's handling characteristics.

▶ *MAST FEET AND EXTENSIONS*

The so-called mast foot actually incorporates several different components: the socket, plug and mast-base.

The form of the plug itself is predetermined by the mast-socket or track built into your particular board. When the plug is connected to the board it should be firm to prevent the rig coming out in use.

The universal joint is fairly standard, consisting of a rubber of plastic form with a threaded pin at each end. These joints do have a habit of breaking after long use, so it's wise to always carry a spare *and* the necessary tools to transfer the plug and mast post to the new joint.

The mast-post connects directly into the base of the mast (or mast extension). It should be a close fit. The unit is normally plastic and has recently incorporated integral pulleys to achieve the downhaul purchase needed for modern sails.

The mast foot and extension are often incorporated into the same structure — the extension is used to lengthen or shorten the mast to accommodate the varying luff lengths of different sized sails.

Mast extensions are generally made of aluminium in order to keep weight to a minimum. They come in two forms, either fixed or adjustable, the latter being more useful. Extensions are adjusted in various common ways. The long extension with adjustable collet can be positioned into a hole at the required

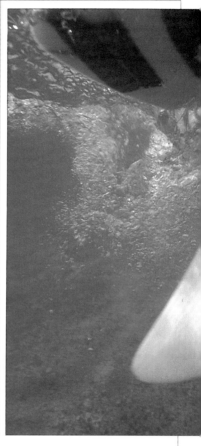

▶ *Right* Mast extensions. One possibility is an extension that is adjusted by use of rubber rings that sit in a choice of grooves. Once in the chosen groove, the collar locks onto the ring. A second ring is placed above the collar, so preventing it moving up and down.

1 *Middle right* A good fin will have no bubbles travelling down it while in use. A small amount of turbulence may exist along the trailing edge.

2 *Below right* Most boards now incorporate a fin-box type fitting into which the majority of fins will fit. If you break or lose a fin a replacement should be easily available.

3 *Far right* The fenced fin is in profile similar to the dolphin. The purpose of the fence is to overcome the old problem of cavitation. The theory is that as air travels down the fin, it is temporarily blocked by the fence and directed off the trailing edge.

height. A split ring can be used if so desired. A collar sits on top of the pin, and the mast is slid onto it. An adjustable extension is particularly useful if sail-to-deck clearance has to be altered.

▶ FINS

The function of a fin or skeg is to give a board directional stability and act as a pivot during turns. A good fin should fulfil a few basic criteria. In the first place the fin should be the right size — long boards require quite a large fin in order to have enough resistance and stability for upwind work. Shorter boards travelling at higher speeds need less fin area since the faster the board travels the greater the resistance gained.

Any fin worth its salt should be laterally stiff. The flexing quality of a fin can be manually tested and if found to be excessive, the fin should be rejected.

The grip offered by the fin is also a primary concern. If the fin does not grip when pressured, the board will lose its directional stability. This process is known as "spin-out" and only occurs while planing. The reason for spin-out is cavitation — bubbles trav-

elling down the fin and disrupting its water contact .

To further combat cavitation, be sure that your fin is in good order and a tight fit in its box. If there are any nicks or pieces broken off, then avoidable turbulence will occur. If possible, repair any damage — or replace the fin. The majority of fins are moulded from plastics although hand-made fibreglass versions are available at a price. New fins sometimes have a sharp lip on both edges as a result of the moulding process. This lip should be sanded down to prevent you cutting yourself should a wipe-out occur.

Good fins are profiled in a shape reminiscent of the leeward side of a sail. This profile gives the fin maximum efficiency and continuity of water-flow over its surface. It is sometimes confusing to establish which type of fin is compatible with a particular type of board. If your board does not have a fin-box type arrangement a replacement skeg may well be obtainable only from the board manufacturer.

Fin progression has kept pace with board design with the fin shapes changing comparatively quickly. The traditional *dolphin-shaped* fin is still frequently seen, as is the *fenced* fin, the first development from

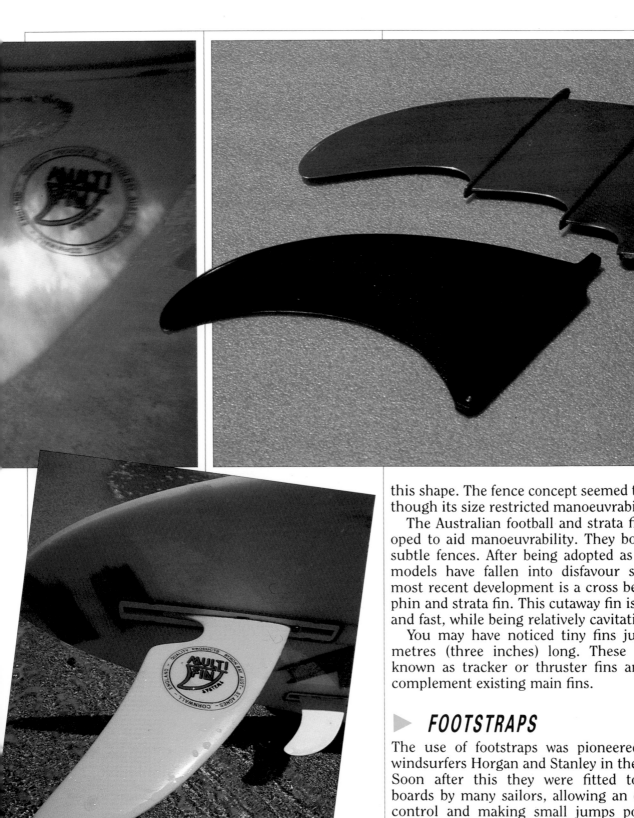

this shape. The fence concept seemed to work well although its size restricted manoeuvrability somewhat.

The Australian football and strata fins were developed to aid manoeuvrability. They both incorporate subtle fences. After being adopted as a trend, these models have fallen into disfavour somewhat. The most recent development is a cross between the dolphin and strata fin. This cutaway fin is manoeuvrable and fast, while being relatively cavitation-free.

You may have noticed tiny fins just eight centimetres (three inches) long. These small fins are known as tracker or thruster fins and are used to complement existing main fins.

▶ FOOTSTRAPS

The use of footstraps was pioneered by Hawaiian windsurfers Horgan and Stanley in the late seventies. Soon after this they were fitted to conventional boards by many sailors, allowing an extra degree of control and making small jumps possible. By the 1980s a high wind board was deemed outmoded if it had no straps.

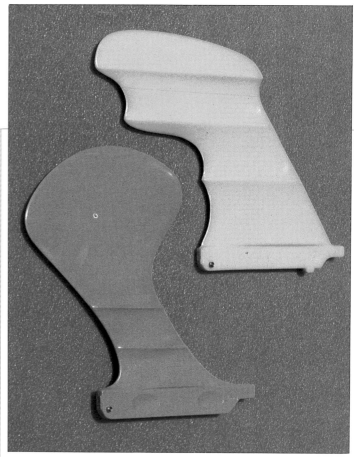

Today almost all new boards are fitted with — or have the facility to fit — footstraps. The only place where footstraps have *not* made an appearance is in Division II racing. The widespread adoption of footstraps is a reflection of improved windsurfing standards. A keen novice can progress in a matter of months into basic footstrap positions. With the use of straps on inland *or* surf waters, footsteering becomes a practical possibility.

The composition of the straps themselves has improved greatly since the early days, mainly due to research and development by companies such as Hy-Jumpers and DaKine. However the standard of footstraps on some production boards is not as high as it should be, a consequence, no doubt, of trying to keep costs down. This is particularly apparent at the cheaper end of the board market where many a footstrap is prone to excessive twisting and flopping. The characteristics of a footstrap may not seem tremendously important to a beginner but any sailor who gets to an intermediate stage will soon realise exactly *how* important they really are.

The perfect strap should maintain a stable shape. A floppy strap will tend to collapse, and make foot-insertion almost impossible. The strap must not be so firmly arched that it will not collapse when you inadvertently tread on it during a manoeuvre. Comfort is an often neglected factor so be sure that the footstrap cover is soft. A soft cover will not fub the top of your feet when sailing barefoot. The strap should be easily adjustable, particularly important if you decide on the spur of the moment to put boots on.

Instances do occur in sailing when you apply excessive pressure on the strap. When beating to windward or riding a short board the strap should flex a little to accommodate a twisted foot position. A bad strap will give out under excessive pressure.

For the strap to fit correctly it needs to be tight over the bridge of your foot. If the fitting is too tight your toes will not appear through the other side. Board balance will be affected as your rear foot will not be over the centreline. If this happens the strap must be lengthened. If the strap is too loose, you could possibly twist an ankle. If your foot can be moved around freely within the strap, then the strap length must be reduced.

Long boards in particular will have a series of straps. The front ones are for light planing conditions and the rear ones for stronger airs. Unless you can handle the board competently in a Force two, do not use the straps — indeed, you would do better to take

4 *Above* The football and strata fins. Football fins were developed by the Hawaiian Shaper, Doug Mann. Because the area of the base is reduced and the area of the tip is increased, the fin is less prone to cavitation.

5 *Bottom far right* The modern fins shown here have a variety of uses. The longer fin on the left is particularly good for long boards. The cutaway fin, although useful on a long board, is better suited to high performance boards.

Right A good strap maintains a firm shape. The cover can be easily removed and the strap itself adjusted with the aid of velcro. To keep the strap arched, a layer of plastic is built into the cover, so that the strap may return to its former position after being trodden on.

6 *Left* Tracker fins are used primarily on funboards, and give extra grip in high speed turns.

them off in order to clear the deck and to reduce the temptation of moving too far back on the board at this stage. Correct footstrap use relies on your effective sailing stance. A sailor who can transfer his bodyweight effectively through the mast foot can use the straps to good effect in light conditions.

Once you get familiar with strap use, steering is transformed into effortless fun and the skill will stand you in good stead for the future.

▶ WEATHER

The world's weather is structured into defined areas of latitude. Both northern and southern hemispheres have corresponding areas although the weather structure varies slightly. For the purposes of this chapter it is the northern hemisphere that will concern us.

GLOBE AND FRONTAL LATITUDES

Over the equator lies a low pressure area characterised by rising hot air. In weather-terms this area is best known as the doldrums, noted for their variable winds and thunderstorms. Winds are drawn in to fill the low pressure zone, commonly giving rise to a north-east trade wind. These trades, although constant, are frequently affected and complicated by depressions.

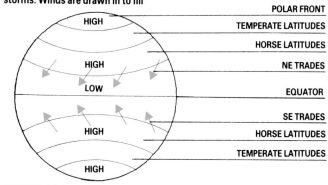

In the mid-latitudes of the northern hemisphere the weather pattern can be conveniently thought as a continuing struggle between cold and warm air masses. These temperate latitudes lie between the high of the horse latitudes, which is created by the movement of the north east trades and the high of the polar fronts. Depressions are created from both regions as air masses arrive into the "depression corridor" of the temperate latitudes. This produces a zone of highly changeable weather which affects Europe, North America and the Atlantic coasts. On the other hand, during the summer the American Pacific coast is normally under the influence of an anti-cyclone (high) centred over the North Pacific. This high produces relatively settled weather.

The differing air-masses of the northern hemisphere tend to remain divided by boundary surfaces known as fronts. It is along the line of these fronts that depressions are first formed, when a mass of warm air pushes into a cold sector.

In an attempt to equalize the atmospheric pressure air is continually on the move, pouring into a low and

---

FRONTAL DEVELOPMENT

On a weather map such as those shown on television weather forecasts the depth or steepness of a depression, and indeed the high of an anticyclone, is indicated by the spacing between the isobars which rather resemble contour lines on a map. Just as a land-based map uses contour lines to join areas of equal height above sea level, so the weather map uses isobars to join points of similar barometric pressure. The weather maps generally show isobars at intervals of four millibars.

---

out of a high pressure region. The rotation of the earth causes deflection of this moving air. This effect is commonly experienced in the temperate climates. The wind pattern around a high or low manifests itself in a spiral effect. In the northern hemisphere, the spiral is *clockwise* and *outwards* around a high pressure area. Correspondingly, around a low pressure area it is *anticlockwise* and *inwards*.

The wind itself is obviously of most importance to us as windsurfers. In meteorological terms the wind is that basic movement of air flowing from high to low pressure. The wind represented on a weather map can be said to blow along the direction of the isobars,

---

DEFLECTION OF WINDS

Differences in wind patterns about highs and lows in the northern and southern hemispheres, caused by the earth's rotation.

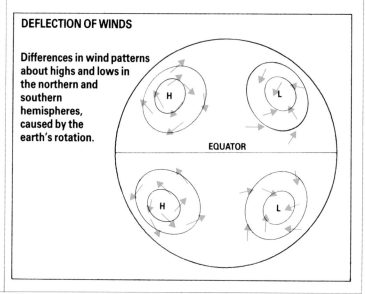

although strictly speaking at low pressures the wind is deflected inwards slightly, and at high pressures it is deflected away from the centre. Directly at the centre of a depression (this is termed cyclonic) there is very little, if any, wind.

Wind is defined by its direction and strength. The direction is always that from which the wind blows. The strength of the wind depends on the speed of the air-movement, given in either metres per second, miles per hour, or knots. The wind is measured on the Beaufort scale, a system devised by Admiral Beaufort in 1805.

The criteria for measuring wind-strengths at sea have to be modified for conditions nearer the shore.

Closely correlated with the wind-force is the state of the sea, involving two components — the first being wind-formed waves, the second being swell or transmitted wave-action. The former effect is localized, whereas the latter may be caused by conditions hundreds of miles away. The waves formed by swell are not steep, but are long and undulating. Wind-blown wave faces tend to be steeper.

In shallow water the wave crests are forced closer together, resulting in an increase in wave-height and steepness. This action results in breaking waves which can reach a fair height.

Wind speed can be measured easily and relatively accurately with an anemometer. The direction of the

Beaufort Scale	Map Symbol	Description	Wind Speed (Knots)	Sea Characteristics
0	⊙	calm	less than 1	Limp sail, mirror-smooth sea
1		light air	1–3	Small ripples. Leaves on trees rustle
2		light breeze	4–6	Small wavelets with smooth crests, tree branches move
3		gentle breeze	7–10	Large wavelets, crests starting to break
4		moderate breeze	11–16	Small waves, a few white caps
5		fresh breeze	17–21	Longer moderate waves; frequent white caps
6		strong breeze	22–27	Large waves begin to form
7		near gale	28–33	Sea heaps up; white foam; trees bend. Small boats head for harbour
8		gale	34–40	Moderately high waves of great length; foam blown in marked streaks
9		strong gale	41–47	High waves; dense foam streaks; crests roll over. Boats heave to
10		storm	48–55	Very high waves with overhanging crests; surface largely foam covered. Visibility decreasing
11		severe storm	56–63	Exceptionally high waves; sea completely foam covered
12		hurricane	64–71	Air filled with spray, visibility seriously affected

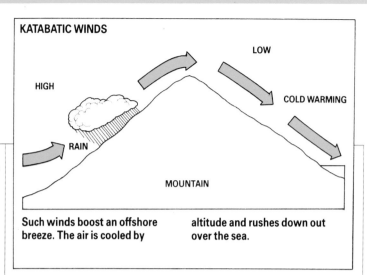

KATABATIC WINDS

Such winds boost an offshore breeze. The air is cooled by altitude and rushes down out over the sea.

wind, however, is more difficult to ascertain — particularly out at sea, where there are no easy means of deducing the direction of the true wind. It is difficult to formulate wind direction merely by looking at the sea. Pay more attention to foam streaks, as a combination of wind-formed waves and swell can often mislead the observer. Wave-direction will *not* directly follow a change in wind-direction.

On no account should the direction of the cloud movement be used as a guide to the true wind. The wind at cloud level often differs markedly in direction and speed from surface wind.

Differing sea-areas have their own wind systems. The most apparent of these are land and sea breezes, trade winds, katabatic winds and monsoons.

Land and sea breezes always blow along coastlines. In fine weather a localized low pressure will build up over the land as a result of the land heating up. An onshore breeze is thus a common feature of hot countries in the afternoon.

In the evening the breeze dies away as the temperature difference between land and sea equalizes. During the night the more rapid cooling of the land produces the reverse effect. A local high forms and the wind flows out to sea, creating a land breeze.

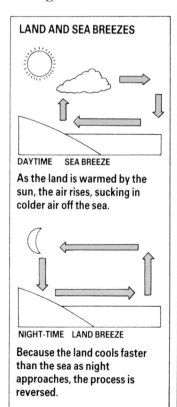

LAND AND SEA BREEZES

DAYTIME　SEA BREEZE

As the land is warmed by the sun, the air rises, sucking in colder air off the sea.

NIGHT-TIME　LAND BREEZE

Because the land cools faster than the sea as night approaches, the process is reversed.

The effect of land and sea breezes is only perceptible when the overall weather pattern is calm. For example, if the wind is westerly Force four during the daytime, a sea breeze may strengthen the existing wind up to Force six. During the night the reverse effect will decrease the wind strength to Force two. However the wind's predominant direction will remain westerly.

Trade winds occur only over sea areas or around coastlines. They arise in approximate latitudes of 30° to 35° north and south. A trade wind is distinguishable by its consistency, and is so called because each was regarded as so dependable by early commercial mariners. Trades are generally associated with fine weather, holding average wind speeds between 7 and 21 knots.

Reliable trade winds can be found in the northern hemisphere, consistently blowing in favourite windsurfing venues such as Hawaii, the Caribbean and the Canary Islands.

Katabatic winds arise when the general airflow passes over a range of hills or high mountains. As the airflow rises the moisture content is precipitated as rain on the windward slopes of the hills. The airflow is rapidly cooled as it passes over the upper slopes of the hills. It then travels down the lee slope accelerating as it goes, heating up with increased pressure as it descends. The air then pours out over the area at the foot of the hills in the form of a strong breeze of relatively low humidity. Such wind are found the world over; the fohn wind over the Alps, and the Mistral in southern France are examples.

Winds of this type can be caused by relatively small changes in pressure distribution. A light breeze passing over the windward side of a hill can become strong to gale force on the leeward side. In areas subject to this type of weather (mainly coasts near to mountains), the sailor should be constantly aware of katabatic wind-formation as it often strikes without warning.

The monsoon wind is an extension of land and sea breeze, but occurs less frequently — usually twice a year. This wind is caused by the distribution of land

and sea around the Indian sub-continent. The cooling of the land mass in the winter leads to the development of a large high-pressure zone over the land, causing a strong land breeze in its turn. In the summer the reverse effect tends to occur. The sea breeze, however, can reach Force 8 and brings with it heavy precipitation. The winter monsoon is dry coming as it does from continental masses. Its average speed is about Force four. Monsoon winds do occur in other areas, such as the north coast of Australia and the western coast of north America.

▶ FORECASTING

Trying to forecast the weather is possibly one of the most difficult skills a windsurfer has to master. Meteorology is one of the trickiest sciences — or arts — known to man. However there are certain sequences of events that can help us to form a forecast.

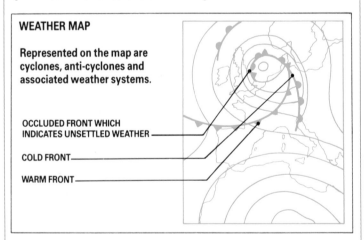

WEATHER MAP

Represented on the map are cyclones, anti-cyclones and associated weather systems.

OCCLUDED FRONT WHICH INDICATES UNSETTLED WEATHER

COLD FRONT

WARM FRONT

When reading a weather map remember that it depicts the situation as it existed several hours ago. Only by analyzing a series of successive weather-maps can you build up a picture of a developing weather pattern. There are a few important rules to follow:
1. A low always moves towards the area where the air-pressure falls most rapidly.
2. A low intensifies when the air pressure in front of it falls more than it rises behind it.
3. A low fills when the air-pressure ahead of it falls less than it rises behind it.
4. Depressions slow down in their east to west progress over land — as a result they can even become stationary.
5. Anti-cyclones determine the path of lows. A low (or several, one after the other) passes the strongest

high in the direction of its circulation, i.e. on the side nearest the pole.
6. A high always moves towards the area where the pressure rises most strongly.

By keeping an eye on both the temperature and the barometric pressure anyone can get some indication of the impending weather. For example, in summer falling temperatures indicate bad weather and rising temperatures mean good weather. However, in winter falling temperatures indicate good weather and rising temperatures indicate bad weather. As for barometric pressure, slowly falling pressure indicates the approach of a large depression or a low — bad weather. Rapidly falling pressure (one millibar per hour) indicates danger of gales or thunderstorms. Slowly rising pressure indicates the approach or build-up of an extensive anti-cyclone or high — good weather. A fast rise denotes the passage of a ridge. It does *not* necessarily mean good weather.

The weather affecting land-locked water is very different from that affecting the sea. You'll find more calms inland than you will on the open beach; the reason is attributable in part to the frictional drag of the land on the wind and the effect of *inversions*. These are layers of warm air which get left anywhere up to a thousand feet high when the sun goes down; and which act like a blanket on the wind, making it very sluggish. So even though weather maps may show isobars close together over one area, it may be absolutely calm overnight as the wind left beneath the inversion layer will have lost all its momentum in colliding with ground objects. That is why the wind drops in the evening and may not reappear until the sun is well up.

This nightly quieting of wind is just one part of the normal way in which the wind changes during a typical day. The "other half" of the daily wind-variation concerns the way that once it begins to pick up it does so steadily, until it reaches its maximum strength during the middle of the afternoon.

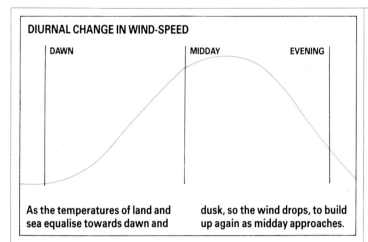

DIURNAL CHANGE IN WIND-SPEED

DAWN   MIDDAY   EVENING

As the temperatures of land and sea equalise towards dawn and dusk, so the wind drops, to build up again as midday approaches.

▶ TIDES AND CURRENTS

Tides can be described in terms of vertical movements of the water — the rising and falling of the sea-level — and horizontal movements of the water, tidal streams or currents. These movements take place with a regular rhythm, and are reliant on gravitational effects of the moon and the sun, the moon's force being the greater. The rate at which tide flows varies from place to place is mainly dependent on the shape, area and depth of the sea bed.

The greatest water level in one cycle is called *high water* (H.W.), the lowest is called *low water* (L.W.). The stage between L.W. and H.W. during which the water rises is the *flood*. The stage between H.W. and L.W. during which the water level falls is the *ebb*.

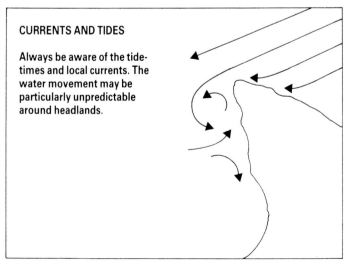

CURRENTS AND TIDES

Always be aware of the tide-times and local currents. The water movement may be particularly unpredictable around headlands.

In the U.K. and Europe tides tend to be "semi-diurnal". They oscillate between H.W. and L.W. twice every lunar day (24 hours 50 minutes), and the height

of successive high and low waters is very nearly the same, as is the time between the high and the low — about 6 hours and 12 minutes.

Ebb and flood together make one tide. If the sun and moon are in conjunction and their gravitational pull coincides (as is the case at full and new moon), tides have their highest rise and lowest fall. These are known as *spring tides*. When the moon is in its first or last quarter, tides have their smallest rise and fall, and are known as *neap tides*.

Tidal currents are the result of the horizontal movement of the water as caused by the tides. When applied to inshore waters the inward flow is known as the flood current, and the outward flow is known as the ebb current. The short time between is known as slack water. The direction and strength of currents will depend on a number of factors — whether the tide is in ebb or flood, spring or neap, the lie of the land, etc. However, there are no general rules and the effects will vary from beach to beach around a coastline. To find out more about the currents you should consult a tide atlas, or get expert local advice.

Obviously, as spring tides involve the greatest movement of water, they therefore flow faster than neaps. The rate of flow will be least in the first and final (sixth) hour of a tide and greatest in the third and fourth hours.

Tide-tables give the predicted times and heights of high and low water for each day of the year for a number of major ports or reference stations. They also give tabulated information on time and height-differences for a large number of secondary ports or sub-stations.

▶ WHEN TO SAIL

Windsurfers can avoid dangerous mistakes by using a little common sense and a few rough guidelines. Before venturing out, find out the times of high and lower water (tide-tables can be purchased from chandleries and windsurfing shops), alternatively the time of the high tide will often be published in the local daily paper. Find out about local rips, found where water is forced through a narrow channel or round a headland, as these can be particularly dangerous when out sailing. If the tides takes you upwind, be thankful; if it takes you downwind, beware. You must learn to recognize when a tide changes from an ebb to a flood or vice-versa.

At low tide many beaches are gently shelving. This means you have a long walk over the sand, but waves

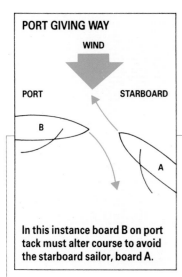

PORT GIVING WAY

In this instance board B on port tack must alter course to avoid the starboard sailor, board A.

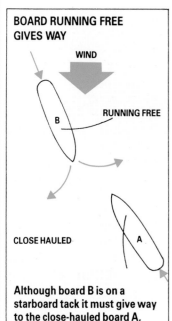

BOARD RUNNING FREE GIVES WAY

Although board B is on a starboard tack it must give way to the close-hauled board A, also on starboard.

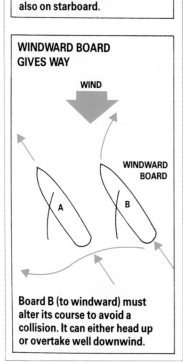

WINDWARD BOARD GIVES WAY

Board B (to windward) must alter its course to avoid a collision. It can either head up or overtake well downwind.

will be small and no problems should be encountered when launching or coming ashore. At high tide the same beaches may shelve steeply, this creates dumping waves that crash on the shoreline making conditions difficult. Beware of the undertow.

When the tide flows in the same direction as the wind (or wind with tide) the water will be smooth. When the tide turns and flows against the wind (wind against tide) the sea will rapidly build up into short, steep waves, making conditions more difficult.

Safety at sea has always been of paramount importance to any kind of sailor and windsurfing is no exception to this rule. The sheer number of people flocking to the water poses an ever-growing problem to the rescue services.

Unfortunately, many windsurfers venture out to sea with inadequate instruction and knowledge of the conditions. Many have a feeble grasp of the principles of safe water use, and far too little respect for the mighty sea itself. However, if the basic rules of safety are adhered to then the sea can be a safe playground and not a treacherous unknown quantity.

▶ *CODES OF CONDUCT*

Getting involved in a collision is a very rude introduction to the rules of sailing. The fact that you may be insured against damage will not prevent you from angering other sailboarders should you recklessly run into another water user.

To the novice, confusion reigns in the majority of cases. This is probably due to a lack of understanding of a few basic rules relating to rights of way. While racing, these rights can be extremely complex, but luckily for leisure purposes a simplified version is quite easy to understand.

The fundamental rule is IYRU rule no. 36 "*a port tack yacht shall keep clear of a starboard tack yacht*" — the explanation for frequent shouts of "starboard!" often heard on the water. A sailor calling "starboard!" is merely claiming his right of way and you should alter course to respect this. As a general guide, if your right hand is nearest to the mast then you are on a starboard tack, and have right of way.

Collision can still occur whilst two craft are on a similar tack. The rule here is again simple. "*The board running free (on a broad reach or run) should give way to the board sailing close-hauled*". The broader positioned board is deemed to have greater scope for control in changing direction than the close hauled craft.

The last basic right of way rule again concerns two boards travelling on a similar tack. This rule is particularly relevant for those wishing to burn off their friends! *"The board windward should keep clear".* If you are sailing to windward, you must stay well clear even if this means that you have to luff up and stop. A better solution is to alter course behind the other craft and overtake to leeward.

These basic rules are required reading for the leisure sailor. A racing sailor will have more studying to undertake if he or she wishes to understand more complex situations.

If in the future you intend to sail on surf, don't be surprised to find the IYRU rules ignored. Surf-sailing has its own generally recognized rights of way. Briefly, a sailor going out through the surf has priority over all those travelling in. If both parties are riding the same wave, a sailor to windward can claim the right to bottom turn. However, a sailor at the critical section holds control of the wave.

Unfortunately, another rule of the road often broken, this time not by the boardsailor, is the one concerning powered craft: *"a craft under power should give way to a craft under sail."* Realistically, it should read, "large vessels will not always alter course for the sake of a windsurfer, nor in all conscience should they be expected to do so". The best advice in this respect is to keep clear of all water users. No problems can then arise.

▶ *COMMON SENSE*

Before going out on the water there are certain points that should be considered. A few moments' thought at this stage will ensure that you get the most out of the sport — windsurfing is very safe so long as you exercise a little common-sense caution.

Check the forecast for the area. This may be obtained from numerous sources; for example the radio and television teletext offer a shipping or marine forecast which is fairly informative about the general weather picture. There are also marine services serving most coastal areas, generally giving recorded messages covering the next 24 hours. Local airports and coastguards have to be aware of the coming weather and generally are quite ready to share their information. In the UK, *Marinecall* and *Weathercall* are perhaps the most specialist recorded forecasts for windsurfers, run by the RYA and the Meteorological Office respectively. Numbers should be available from your local exchange.

Be sure to tell someone where you are going, and more importantly, what time you expect to be back. If you should get into difficulty they may then be in a position to raise the alarm. Don't forget to report back to this person as rescue services have enough to do without searching for a sailor who is safe and warm at home. It is not advisable to sail alone. Try and sail with a friend, as another sailor can often get you out of trouble.

Make sure all your equipment is suitable and in a seaworthy condition. Wear appropriate clothing which will keep you warm and clearly visible at all times, not forgetting your buoyancy aid. All your equipment must be in good order — it costs nothing to check it regularly. Pay particular attention to all lines and mast-foot fittings. If anything appears remotely worn, replace it immediately. Always use a safety leash connecting the rig to the board, and remember that you can buy devices that enable you to sail home should your UJ break.

Distress signals should be carried, ideally in the form of flares. In addition, a dayglo flag — often carried in the mast — may alert onlookers. A whistle may also be used to draw attention to yourself. Make sure, however, that it is easily accessible. A spare length of line can often be a life-saver, you can use it either for towing someone else or for effecting emergency repairs. Wherever possible, these small items should be attached to your person, and not to your equipment in case of separation.

Avoid offshore winds and strong tidal areas. Offshore winds can be extremely hazardous; although the sea appears calm inshore, further offshore the wind can be much stronger. Consider other water users. Windsurfing is most often recreational but other water users may actually be at work, so keep clear of shipping lanes and other restricted areas.

Above all, be realistic about your own sailing capabilities in the prevailing conditions. Use a sail which you know you can handle — and if in doubt, don't go out! Let common sense prevail at all times.

▶ *HYPOTHERMIA*

Cold air and cold water can combine in certain circumstances to affect the body's core temperature. Even in warmer climates, prolonged exposure to wind can cause a dangerous lowering of body temperature. Beware of sailing in winter especially in cold climates. The onset of *hypothermia* (suffering from cold) is a real threat to every sailor who braves the cold condi-

tions. Hypothermia is more than just feeling cold — your hands can withstand a severe drop in temperature, but your torso cannot. A small drop in temperature around the vital organs can be fatal.

The sailor must be able to recognize the symptoms of hypothermia. The first stage is a loss of awareness followed quickly by a loss of co-ordination in the hands and feet. The next step is more easily recognized, namely shivering. At this point the victim must be returned to the shore. If the body temperature drops much further, the heart and brain will become oxygen-starved and cease to function. The best medicine is prevention. If you or a friend feel a little cold then get out of the water and into dry clothes. The first priority is to get warm so take a warm drink and raise your body temperature by taking a warm, not hot, bath. Know your limits — if you are unfit you are more susceptible to being caught out.

In exceptionally warm climates the opposite effect, called *hyperthermia*, can occur. This is generally due to wearing a wet suit that is too warm, meaning that the sailor will quickly dehydrate. Again, you will not realize what is happening, so think sensibly before going afloat.

▶ SELF RESCUE

No matter how competent you are you can still find yourself in trouble. Sometimes the only option left is to rescue yourself. There are various ways of getting into self-unexpected trouble. The novice is particularly susceptible to sailing in conditions way beyond his or her ability. One situation which can be easily avoided is sailing for too long and becoming physically exhausted. If you *are* feeling a little weary, play safe, and get back to dry land.

These things can be avoided, but many common mishaps are unpredictable. Equipment failure and deteriorating conditions are two of the commonest ways of getting into trouble. The weather forecast can be inaccurate, the wind can pick up in a few minutes, or completely change direction. The moral is not to venture out too far. If such a situation arises and you can no longer sail, you must be prepared and have an alternative method of getting home. Do not hesitate, as this may only compound the danger. Proceed straight into the self-rescue routine, to paddle for the shore.

If you can't manage to fold the sail away, paddling may become severely hampered. If progress towards

1 *Top* Sitting on your board with your back to the wind, remove the mast foot from the board. Work along the foot of the sail and release the outhaul.

2 *Above* Remove all battens from the sail and position the boom towards the top of the mast. The sail can now be rolled towards the mast from its trailing edge. You may use the uphaul and outhaul to tie the boom and sail securely to the mast.

3 *Above* Completing the self rescue procedure. While kneeling on the board, position the rig under you and lie on top of it. You can now paddle comfortably towards the shore.

the shore is restricted, you must cut any financial losses and dump the rig. The board will be easier to paddle without the rigging. The golden rule is never to leave the board. If you are stranded, it can act as a life-raft and keep you afloat.

If you are making no progress, you may need to attract attention to yourself. If no flares or other safety features are available, you must use the international distress signal.

▶ *AIDED RESCUE*

Sailors with a modicum of ability should be capable of assisting a fellow-sailor in distress. If in doubt as to your ability, go to shore for extra help. If someone is spotted struggling then waste no time. Proceed to their rescue immediately.

Try and pull up alongside the stranded boardsailor. If his or her rig is not already packed away, help to de-rig while both sitting on your respective boards. With your board heading homeward, position the other sailor's board directly alongside.

When you get close to the shore, do not dump the rescued sailor. Make sure he/she gets to dry land. In circumstances where the sailor is in extreme distress, or seems panic-stricken (as perhaps a child might be) do not leave your board. A panicking victim, no matter how small, can easily, if inadvertently, drown you.

◀ The distress signal is understood by the whole of the sailing and shipping fraternity. To attract attention, wave your arms up and down next to your body. If you are spotted, a craft will immediately come to your aid.

▲ Aided rescue. The sailor to be rescued should lie on his/her own board in the manner appropriate for self-rescuing. He should then hold the base of your mast in which position he or she can be readily towed.

In strong winds and waves, jumps are almost unavoidable.

Fixing the rig to the board as shown is quick and efficient.

HIGHER WIND SAILING

Funboarding is a general term used to describe the use of any high-wind performance equipment. The emphasis is placed on the element of fun derived from sailing in winds in excess of Force four. The majority of aspiring windsurfers aim to develop the skills necessary to perform in these conditions.

The attractive features of this kind of sailing are self-evident; high speed, rapid changes in direction and various aerial manoeuvres. In higher winds everything happens so fast that one's reaction time is very limited and one must therefore expect a number of spills along with the thrills. High-wind sailing is not at all forgiving; the slightest mistake or loss of balance can lead to an immediate and sometimes spectacular fall.

Although it's entirely feasible to learn to windsurf in light airs on a large funboard, you cannot always apply what you have learned to the hybrid shorter models in the same conditions. Moreover, because stronger winds render the basic sailing techniques redundant, progressing onto a short board is almost like starting from scratch although practice and tech-

nique are still the essential elements for success.

The world's finest exponents of the short boards have honed their skills through months of continual training — usually in warm climates with consistent trade winds. Early pioneers, such as Mike Walte and Matt Schweitzer — who are still regarded as top sailors — are now permanently resident in Hawaii, which for boardsailors represents Mecca. When funboarding first came into its own in the late 1970s it took months to refine manoeuvres which are now considered almost elementary. Once developed, however, and shown to a world-wide public on video-screens, these manoeuvres caught on remarkably quickly. It is now possible, with the aid of instructional books, windsurfing journals and windsurfing videos, to learn the basics of funboarding rapidly and with ease, once longboard competence is established.

PREPARING TO LAUNCH

Ideally, before trekking to the water's edge with masses of equipment, you should walk over to check out the prevailing conditions. In the main, short-

boards under 330 cm (130 inches) in length will not perform unless the wind is fairly constant. Gusty conditions are hard work as the board will go through phases of planing one minute and stalling the next, an experience which is not pleasant and is certainly not an ideal introduction to funboarding. A minimum wind speed dictates whether the equipment being used will plane. Force three to four is sufficient to get 90 per cent of funboards up and away, and is also a reasonable strength for venturing out on your maiden voyage. If the wind is too gusty and happens to lull you may become stranded some distance from the shore. A wind that is too lively may lead to handling problems and a similar end-result.

At this crucial juncture in your windsurfing career you may be unsure as to how strong the wind actually is. The chart correlating the Beaufort scale to visible water characteristics can again be consulted. The chart, of course, is only a guide and if you are still doubtful about the wind-strength you will find an anemometer more reliable. This is a windspeed indicator which measures wind in metres per second and comes in various shapes and sizes. If you don't feel inclined to invest in this kind of high-technology then local advice is the best — ask a sailor who is performing competently in the prevailing conditions. If you explain your situation he or she will have an idea as to whether the conditions are suitable for a funboard beginner.

▶ LAUNCHING

In higher winds it's not as simple as one imagines to transport equipment to the launching area. Dragging the board and rig around will not do its life-expectancy much good. But do not despair there are a variety of ways which make the task of getting your gear to the water's edge easier.

First, for convenience, insert the mast foot into the board in its correct sailing position. Do this in a sheltered spot away from the full force of the wind. What usually happens at this point is that the funboarder nonchalantly picks up his or her gear only to find him or herself blown about by the high wind and dumped in a heap on the sand, still clutching board and rig. So step back, and approach things more systematically. Put one hand on the mast first, just below the boom. The golden rule is to stay to windward of the sail. Any movement will cause the sail to luff, but this should not be too serious, given that the wind in the sail will have little directional force. To

get closer to the board, raise the sail. Because it's still pointing to windward it will probably flap quite violently. Standing on the windward side of the board, bend down and take the windward front footstrap with your spare hand. Your options are now open.

Excess pressure on the sail from your head will eventually lead to distortion in the lower sail area. The latter method reduces this as well as being more comfortable in higher winds.

Instances may arise when a long walk to — or back from — the water is inevitable; the tide may ebb and leave you facing a long walk back to the car. In such cases put the board upside down on top of the sail and lift the whole lot on top of your head. Your legs are now free from board obstruction for the long walk. Think a little before attempting this method — a heavy board could strain more than just your legs.

The time has arrived to approach the water. Proceed relatively slowly as this will help maintain constant control of the ever-flapping rig. When launching in surf, many sailors prefer to stand to leeward of the board as this prevents the board from being taken downwind. Enter the water and keep going until it

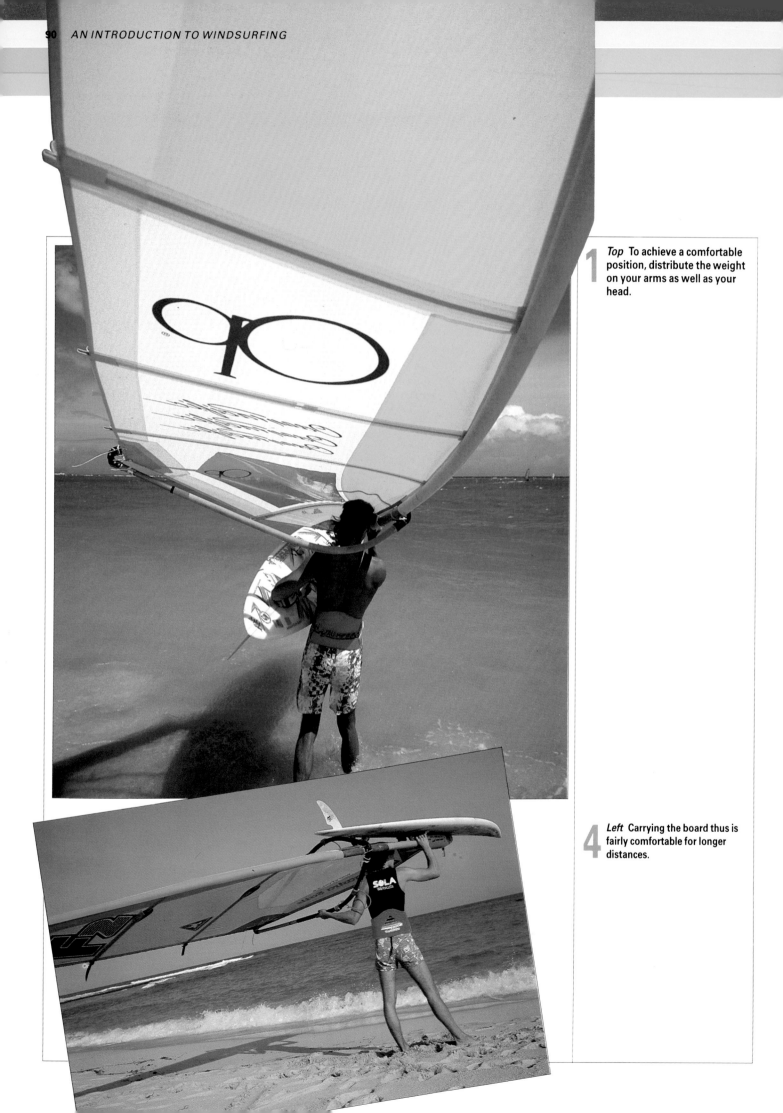

1 *Top* To achieve a comfortable position, distribute the weight on your arms as well as your head.

4 *Left* Carrying the board thus is fairly comfortable for longer distances.

2 *Right* Lift the mast and board vertically, so that the rig rests on your head.

3 *Below* An alternative method is to place the mast along the leeward rail of the deck and then lift.

1 *Above* Lower the board onto the water. To prevent the board from luffing into the wind, maintain forward pressure on the mast foot. Stand next to the board, almost adjacent to the footstraps and keep the board from moving forward so that the rig becomes more upright and suddenly develops plenty of power.

2 *Above right* In one continuous movement place your rear foot on the board, sheet in, then simultaneously step on with your front foot. For an instant ease the rig forward to increase forward motion.

laps around your knees — you can now be sure that there's sufficient depth for the fin.

As you start sailing after a high wind launch sudden acceleration will be experienced as the board is already in a broad-reaching position. All that remains is just to trim to the required point of sailing.

▶ WATERSTARTING

When subjected to high winds you will find it becomes increasingly difficult to uphaul in the conventional manner. The waterstart is a technique initially more difficult but ultimately much easier than trying to heave up the rig against the wind. The ability to waterstart is really the key to funboarding — unless and until you master this technique you cannot really call yourself a funboarder.

When waterstarting, the power of the sail is utilized to lift the sailor bodily out of the water and onto the board. The initial difficulty is learning to control the rig whilst lying in deep water, a feat which puts immense strain on your energy resources until the technique is mastered. Although possible in lighter airs, the waterstart is essentially a high-wind manoeuvre, the prerequisite being a windforce capable of lifting an adult clear of the water. The waterstart is one of the few windsurfing manoeuvres that actually becomes easier as the wind increases. When it is perfected, much time and energy can be saved — vital when coping with big waves, or when racing. A successful waterstart gets you onto the board already in a sailing position, with a powered sail and initial forward motion.

You can waterstart with any board and sail provided that there is enough wind. Life can be made a little

1 *Bottom right* To release the rig from the water, the mast must be to windward of the sail's clew. If it is not, swim to the clew end of the boom and lift it up. The wind will get under the clew and start to increase lift. As it does so, release the boom, and the rig will flip over into the correct position.

2 *Top right* The wind can be used to good effect to help rig release. Pull the front boom-end up and over the board's tail. The wind will funnel under the sail and lift it completely clear.

easier if early practice sessions are carried out in shallow waters. If you can stand up, it's possible to take a short rest without getting your lungs full of water. The shallow waterstart involves considerably less effort than the deep water variety as the difficult rig-positioning can be done with ease and having your feet on the bottom makes it easier to present the sail to the wind. If you take the precaution of using a board you can uphaul with comparative ease, then it should be possible to sail back to the shore if anything goes wrong. A minimum windspeed of twelve knots is recommended for practice as with such a wind a sail bigger than 6 square metres (65 sq ft) should not be needed. A large sail, although it generates a lot of power, is difficult to get out of the water as are fixed profile sails.

Recovering the rig from the water is the most difficult step and often causes great annoyance. After a wipe-out the rig can fall into many different positions. The rig may dive underwater, however, if you swim towards the mast-tip inching along the mast as you go, the rig will re-emerge on the surface. Holding the mast near the front of the boom, use the rig to position the board so that it lies across the wind.

With the rig in one hand, move back up to the mast near the boom, and with your spare hand on the tail of the board, reposition mast and board across the wind.

Occasionally at this stage the clew may stick in so to aid release, force the rig to windward. Whilst treading water to windward, place your rear hand and then your front hand on the boom in their respective positions. You can now attempt the waterstart itself.

The rig should be under control, and in effect, you're on a beam reach. To develop the power needed for lift, the board must be on a slightly broader course. Keep your hands well back on the boom as you would in the beach-start when bearing away. If you edge your hands towards the mast, less sail will be presented to the wind and the board will also tend to luff. As you would in conventional sailing control the rig-power by sheeting in and out with your rear hand. To bear away, push the rig forward; to luff up, pull it back.

When learning to waterstart it is sensible to practice first on good old dry land. Land simulation will give an indication of the forces required to lift your body-weight. The tricky art of rig-control can be learned without the usual two-hour drinking session experienced while in the water. It is much easier to propel your body to an upright position from solid ground than from the water, but basically the principle is the same. When actually venturing into the water a high-buoyancy harness is an asset, especially in the early days. If you must jump in, remember to jump in at the shallow rather than the deep end.

▶ HARNESS TECHNIQUE

Having mastered the waterstart, it should be well within your capabilities to venture out in winds of Force three to four with complete confidence. Unless you are a direct descendant of Charles Atlas even five minutes in these conditions will leave you physically drained. The harness is a simple yet effective device that facilitates sailing for prolonged periods of time — provided it is used correctly. As soon as you have basic rig-control and can avoid being catapulted over the front of the board in every gust of wind, it is time to learn to hook in.

Setting up the harness is a very personal thing. The hook itself can face either up or down and the lines, either long or short, can be placed inside or outside your hands on the boom. The illustrated method is the most commonly used — but feel free to follow your preference.

1 *Top left* When you feel comfortable transfer your rear foot to the rear section of the board. Often you will find that your foot can be positioned directly into the rear strap, providing the wind is strong enough.

Never place your foot any nearer the tail than this or it may sink. Continue to tread water with the front foot. This keeps the rig upright, giving it lift as well as keeping your liquid intake to a minimum.

2 *Middle left* To develop lift, stretch up both arms to expose more sail area to the wind. Simultaneously, try to thrust your body out of the water. The board will now start to sail. Trail your front foot until you are sure you are going to make it onto the board.

3 *Bottom left* With both feet securely on board, level out and plane.

▲ Hooking in. With just a hint of wind, the basic techniques can be rehearsed on dry land. Again this will save energy and hopefully avoid a great deal of frustration.

1 *Right* Setting the harness lines.

2 *Far right* To hook in, bend down and straighten your arms. The actual hooking-in movement is quite rapid, and it may take a while before you can match the line-movement to the correct body-movement.

Place the lines on the boom so that the middle of the line represents the balance point of the rig. To make this easier hold the rig up as if sailing and then grip the centre of the line with one hand. If you're extremely lucky the rig will balance, but the chances are that it will be unstable. If the rig twists forward, move the front harness line ahead towards the mast. Undersheeting requires adjustment of the rear fixing point away from the mast. As you can see, finding the point of balance is a matter of continual trial and error. Usually the line-fixings end up about a shoulder-width apart on the boom. To calculate the drop of the lines, hook in as if sailing. Your hands should be placed on the boom, just outside and equidistant from the harness fixings. This will prevent the lines continually rubbing against your forearms. Keeping body-weight in a backwards direction to prevent catapulting, start the lines swinging by rapidly flexing your arms in unison. You will find that flexing your knees will swing the lines under the hook.

Hooking out is a less complex operation. If you jerk the boom towards you the line will simply drop out. In reasonable wind it is possible when on the water, to direct your whole body-weight through the harness. If the harness is set correctly there will be very little strain on the arms. You will soon be able to release either hand temporarily from the boom, and ultimately, you can release both hands for a split second without mishap.

When sailing hooked in it is imperative to be aware of your surroundings. In a lull you can fall in to windward with the rig on top of you, but more dangerous is the squall; if unbalanced you can be bundled off the deck and physically thrown over the nose of the board. This may be a great source of entertainment for spectators, but the chances of survival without injury are slim. The moral would seem to be — if in doubt, hook out!

▶ *THE CARVE GYBE*

The carve gybe is the classic funboard turn and forms the basis of other well-known funboard manoeuvres. All variations of high-speed fluid turns involve the same concept of turning the board through 180° in a fast, efficient manner. High speed turns do however tend to throw up mental barriers for the short board scholar. If you sit back and analyze the steps involved, the move seems less intimidating.

Certain boards will carve more effectively than others. It is essential to have a board shorter than 330

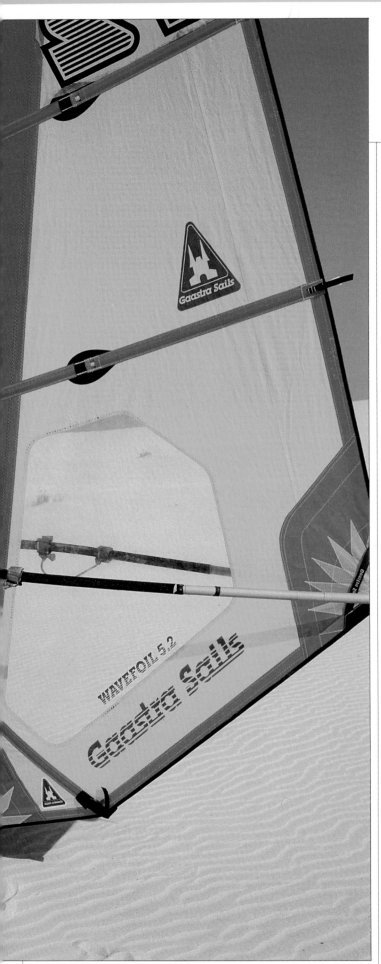

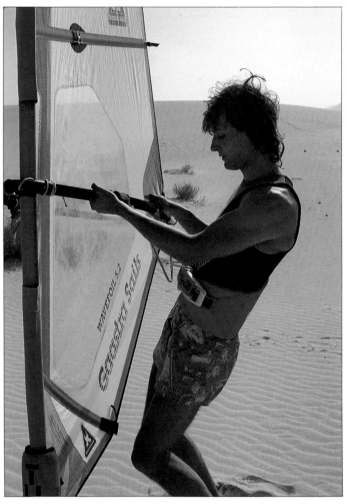

centimetres (130 inches), since the larger funboards with broad, thick tails and chunky rails do tend to stall on entry to this type of turn. Ideally, full planing conditions are required in about a Force four wind. Large sails, above six metres, do tend to make the manoeuvre harder, so use a rig that generates controllable power.

A carve gybe entered at slow speed is actually harder to perform and requires keener balance than one executed at high speed. At the opposite end of the scale a gybe at Mach one is purely make or break — and often results in a wipe-out.

Having completed the carve gybe, instantly reposition what was your front hand to become the new rear hand. The power can be turned on again simply by sheeting in. To complete the gybe all that remains is finally to reposition your feet onto the new tack.

If the correct procedure is followed the carve gybe will be extremely efficient because there is only a short period of time with no power in the sail, therefore board-speed is maintained throughout. First attempts will probably find you committing all sorts of cardinal sins — such as changing the position of your feet during the turn. The result of any mistake is loss of speed. You might find the long drawn out arc easier to accomplish in early attempts, especially on a large board. However, this smooth turn does eat up a lot of space downwind. Practice is again the order of the day, the aim being to progressively tighten the arc whilst still maintaining speed.

Finally, remember that the carve gybe is a continuous fluid manoeuvre which must be broken down on the water into a series of small, step-by-step progressions. The distinguishing mark of this classic turn is not the speed of entry into it, but the speed of exit from it.

1 When fully planing on a reach, choose a patch of flat water for your intended turn, this will prevent unnecessary bouncing of the board. Pick up a little extra speed by bearing away onto a broad reach. When you make the decision to turn, begin to lift the windward rail with your front foot. Remain sheeted in to maintain speed — all speed gained on entry to the gybe, within reason, will make foot-steering sweeter.

Watch the water for signs of gusts and wind-shifts as the harness rather commits your body-weight, enhancing any mistake you may make.

2 As you pass off the broad reach, take the rear foot out of its strap and use it to apply a modicum of pressure on the leeward rail. Avoid any violent body-movement, which could cause the board to kick out of its arc and off the plane. Once the board bites into the turn, it's possible to sheet out a little. This will prevent overpowering further into the turn. The arc followed by the board is dictated by a combination of leaning back and into the turn. Leaning too far either way will cause the rail to dig in. The board will break from the arc and lose momentum. If the sailor is fully committed to the turn the board will carve its own course, passing quickly onto a broad reach on the opposite tack. For a perfect carve gybe, the rig has to be flipped around the nose of the board just prior to entering the new broad-reach mode.

3 To flip the rig, place your front hand near to the front boom end and release your rear hand. Your front hand will not act as a pivot. Because the board is continuously carved onto the new tack through foot pressure alone, the rig will automatically flip itself around through wind-pressure.

▶ THE ONE-HANDED CARVE GYBE

The one-handed gybe, as the name suggests, is purely an extension of the conventional carve-gybe. A short while ago it was regarded purely as a flamboyant gesture, having little practical use in its own right. Recently, however, it has been regarded with more favour and it has come to be regarded as a useful part of the high-wind sailor's repertoire. If approaching the gybe with exceptional speed, or even if over-powered, dragging one hand will maintain a continuous carving motion.

Trailing the hand in the water produces two useful effects. When overpowered during the turn the board has a tendency to break from its arc and shoot recklessly downwind into an irretrievable position. However, leaning in further and digging the hand in the water has the effect of committing the sailor's body-weight fully to the turn, thus preventing the board from "breaking out". The second effect of trailing the hand is that in the latter portion of the turn it will make the arc of the board tighten. If the rider can succeed in staying aboard, he or she will have achieved the ever-elusive tightly-planing gybe.

4 As it swings, be prepared to cross over your rear hand to take the boom on the new tack; this hand now becomes the new front hand.

▲ When midway through the turn, release the rear hand from the boom. Leaning into the turn will enable you to briefly stroke the water. As the sail flips around, return to meet the boom on the new tack.

Funboard Racing

There are a variety of funboard racing styles, and the disciplines vary from event to event. The order of the races depends on the local conditions, as indeed do the types of races that are included in the whole event.

The top rung of the funboard racing ladder is the World Cup. This is run by the World Boardsailors Association (WBA) and involves the world's top-flight professionals. All events in the WBA series are run to an identical format. Top manufacturers subscribe to the racing circuit and competing sailors, who must be members of a manufacturer's team, may only use members' equipment.

To internationalize the sport, each event in the usual series of five is held in a different country. Common venues range from Hawaii to Holland, so that each competitor has a chance to compete on his or her home ground.

The two main disciplines in the World Cup are course racing and slalom. Both run on a minimum windspeed, allowing the highly competitive boards to be fully planing. This is not only good for competition, but is also more entertaining for the spectators. The majority of other funboard events are generally run along similar lines, nearly all involving the same two disciplines.

Course racing represents a tactical approach to funboard racing. Its rules are primarily governed, as in the traditional triangle racing, by the International Yacht Racing Union. The equipment, however, lends itself much more to high performance in strong airs. Course boards of around 3 m 70 cm to 3 m 80 cm (12 ft to 12 ft 4 in) are made as light as possible with the aid of exotic materials such as carbon, kevlar and epoxy. The majority of rigs used are camber-induced to facilitate good upwind performance.

FLATTENED TRIANGLE COURSE

The course used is a development from that used for triangle racing. Any changes made to the course are to suit the characteristics of the funboard. The upwind leg is normally short, as the funboard's main strength is in reaching rather than upwind sailing. To accommodate this, a series of long, exhilarating reaches follow the short upwind section. To test sailor's all-round funboard ability the reaches are combined with a series of gybes in a downwind configuration.

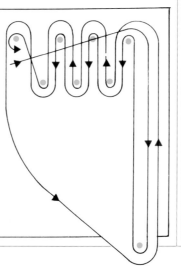

◄ **Left** Approaching a turn at speed does not allow for error. Positions often change at this point.

Below Although the beating leg is short, tactically vast advantages can be gained from it. A course race always starts on an upwind leg. The sailor who gets a clean start is assured of undisturbed wind from other craft enabling him or her to establish a lead.

Scoring is on a points basis. The winner of a race will pick up the least number of points. Often a sailor's worst result can be discarded. The winner is therefore the sailor with the lowest points accumulation after a set number of races; usually a series of five.

The progression of underwater profiles on production funboards is a direct result of research and development carried out by manufacturers to improve their specialised racing boards, and these underwater profiles are designed to make the board plane early at the minimum windspeed. For further excitement, however, the races are continued in strong wind. Certainly the World Cup sailors are capable of handling these extreme conditions, but most funboard events do tend to have quite a high standard of sailing. In the stronger airs a complete race may take as little as twenty minutes. Sometimes the races are run back to back so that even the winning sailor may only just have time to change sails between races.

In circumstances when the wind picks up during a funboard event, the organizers will often switch from course racing to the more high-wind orientated slalom competition. The principles involved in slalom revolve round consecutive reaches and high speed turns. The equipment is again critical. The boards are often less than 3 metres (9 ft 9 in) in length and are especially designed for slalom conditions. The important criterion is that the board should plane early, yet maintain a high top-end speed. The turns cannot be ignored; so the board must also carve-gybe well, otherwise ground is lost at the mark. Successful sailors will keep their boards on the plane continually through the gybe process while being aware of other sailors trying to gybe on an inside line.

There are two popular types of slalom course. The first and most commonly used is the downwind "M" shaped course. The competitors execute a series of broad reaches, finally finishing further downwind on the beach.

The start of a slalom is again a point where a major advantage can be gained. The start can be from the water or directly off the shoreline, the latter being more common.

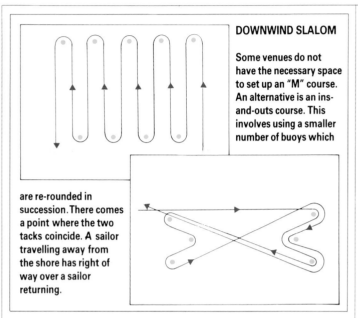

DOWNWIND SLALOM

Some venues do not have the necessary space to set up an "M" course. An alternative is an ins-and-outs course. This involves using a smaller number of buoys which are re-rounded in succession. There comes a point where the two tacks coincide. A sailor travelling away from the shore has right of way over a sailor returning.

In some more localized funboard events long distance racing is also incorporated if the local conditions are suitable. Long distance racing takes a variety of forms, commonly reaching across wide bays or around islands. The advent of funboards has really increased the popularity of long-distance racing. Often held in strong winds, it is a real challenge for sailors to battle against the elements for a few hours. These races are often run separately from other events. A favourite amongst boards and flotillas alike is the Virgin Islands "Hook-In-and-Hold On". The wind-strengths here vary considerably, and the event attracts all standards of windsurfers. Held annually, the race involves hopping between a group of islands. In light winds such an event can take up to ten days or so. The consideration of safety is of course paramount. With adequate rescue facilities this adventurous aspect of windsurfing will hopefully continue to grow.

▶ WAVE SAILING

Wave-sailing is probably the most attractive aspect of windsurfing from a spectator's point of view, and although it sometimes looks impossible, it's open to all sailors once basic short-board techniques are mastered.

It is necessary to have the correct equipment for wave-sailing. Proficient sailors only venture out in strong winds when the manoeuvrability of their sinkers is greatest. The top sailor will use a variety of

boards, usually custom-made to his or her requirements. It is important to have a strong rigging-system, otherwise mistakes will be expensive.

Wave-sailing consists of three main elements — transitions, rides and spectacular jumps. Wave-sailing really originated in Hawaii, where prolonged sailing is possible in ideal conditions of surf, sun and consistent winds. This aspect of sailing has evolved to incorporate many radical manoeuvres. Wave sailing gives the sailor a tremendous amount of scope as his or her imagination can run riot to develop a personal style, with combinations of different manoeuvres. A sailor can push development in any direction he or she desires, be it conservative or radical.

Transitions are ways of changing from tack to tack. Wave sailing's high-flying transitions are developments from the basic manoeuvres described in Chapter 3. There is a large repertoire of gybing modes, including ducking under the sail (duck gybe) and more recently the airborne turn (aerial gybe). Wave boards are difficult to tack. Being low volume boards, they tend to sink when not moving. However, the more acrobatic sailors *can* tack these short boards. A complex tack has recently arrived on the

Opposite top right A custom-board has performance and strength characteristics superior to most production models.

Quick departure from the beach can give an early and sometimes unassailable lead.

The competitors on hearing the gun have to take to the water like lemmings, carrying their equipment as they go. A fast sprint and rapid beach start has obvious advantages.

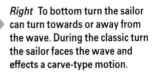

> *Right* To bottom turn the sailor can turn towards or away from the wave. During the classic turn the sailor faces the wave and effects a carve-type motion.

> *Far right* As the board is redirected up the wave-face, the sailor must turn to project the board back down. If left until the last moment, the board can be projected off the lip of the wave.

scene, whereby the sailor again ducks under the sail (duck tack). This is really a progressional manoeuvre, and can take months of practice to perfect.

Practice is certainly the key to success as a wave rider. The sailor's skill can be almost infinitely honed. Riding (surfing) involves a combination of directional changes up and down the wave face. When strung together the turns produce a scalloping-type motion. The turn at the bottom of the face is the *bottom turn*. The corresponding top turn is called a *cut back*.

The riding motions are particularly exhilarating, and indeed addictive to many participants. When timing and control is keenly developed, the board can be projected aerially off-the-lip to re-enter on the same wave. Such a manoeuvre is only a dream for many sailors.

Many rides often result in the overconfident sailor being engulfed in the white water or by the critical section of the wave. If the wave is powerful, the sailor will feel as if he has been tumbled in a washing machine. The effect on the equipment is often devastating.

To the layman jumping is an easily recognizable aspect of wave sailing. With ample wind and a steep wave-face, board and sailor can be projected anything up to 40 feet in the air. The actual jumping process is not overly difficult, the sailor's skill is tested in landing. Once airborne the easy option is to bail out, but a proficient sailor will attempt a more elegant landing.

Jumps can range from a small hop to a huge leap, progressing in difficulty to the elusive aerial loop, which has only ever been pulled off by an elite group

Most wave-sailing is done on a leisure basis, but competitions do exist where the sailors can display their consistency and artistic talent. Events are usually held on a man-to-man knockout basis, with initial heats of ten minutes. The final round is over a prolonged period up to twenty minutes. The winner is the sailor judged to have scored the most points for riding, jumps and transitions.

▶ SPEED-SAILING

Speed-sailing is probably the most highly specialized aspect of windsurfing. The sailor often achieves speeds of 30 knots (around 45 mph). The conditions for speed-sailing are particularly critical. To develop board-speed the wind has to be strong, usually in excess of 25 knots. The strong wind must coincide with flat water, as hitting chop at speed will not only slow the board down, but also make control impossible. All competitive speed-courses are run on the fastest point of sailing, the reach. A tight beam-reach of 90° to the wind is slower than a broader reach, the ideal bearing being 110° to 120° off the wind. As may be imagined, perfect conditions do not occur all that often during competition. To increase the chances of good conditions the more competitive courses are set up in places with a reputation for high winds, with wind funnelling offshore, thus reducing the fetch of any wind-blown chop.

To achieve a fast time it is vital to have the very latest equipment. The rigs used are all of hard profile, incorporating many battens. There is much

GLOSSARY

Apparent wind — a wind felt whilst in motion, the direction of which is determined by the speed of the boat.

A.B.S. — a plastic material from which some production boards are manufactured.

Bailing out — abandoning the board, usually in surf situations.

Battens — fibreglass strips that help to hold the sail profile.

Bearing — an angle determined from a fixed point or observer.

Beating — a point of sailing upwind.

Camber — the curvature of the sail.

Carve — turning the board on its inside rail, usually while bottom turning or gybing.

Cavitation — a process during which the skeg becomes aerated causing it to lose grip.

Centre of effort — the centre point of the sail area where the forces of wind pressure are concentrated.

Centre of lateral resistance — centre point of the underwater area of the hull, usually the daggerboard.

Clear wind — wind that reaches the sail without prior interference.

Cleat — mechanical holding for lines.

Cross-shore — a wind-direction running along the shoreline.

Custom board — a hand produced board, usually made to the sailor's own specification.

Downhaul — line attached to the foot or tack of the sail, producing tension on the luff area.

Dry suit — completely sealed costume with little or no water penetration.

Hull — the board itself, excluding the rig.

Inhaul — the piece of line holding the boom to the mast.

I.Y.R.U. — International Yacht Racing Union.

Knots — nautical miles per hour. A nautical mile is 6080 feet, or 1853 metres.

Latitude — distance from the equator (north or south) measured in degrees.

Leech — the sail area between the clew and the head.

Leeward — a direction away from the wind.

Luff — the sail area running parallel and adjacent to the mast.

Nose — the front of the board (the "bow" in nautical terms).

Eye of the wind — the exact point from which the true wind is coming.

Extensions — varying sized pieces of "tubing" used to alter the length of masts and booms.

Fetch — the distance wind-induced water has to travel uninterrupted.

Fibreglass — a material commonly used in the construction of high-performance boards.

Flare — sinking the tail of a long board when gybing.

Foil — the cross-sectional thickness of a skeg or daggerboard.

Footstraps — webbing loops for foot insertion in high wind and surf situations.

Gybe — turning the board downwind.

Head — the upper section of the sail.

Heading — the direction in which a craft is travelling.

Hitch — a simple knot used to make a line fast to an object.

Offshore — away from the land e.g. offshore wind.

Outhaul — a line attached to the clew used to trim the camber of the sail.

Planing — when the board rises up and reaches speeds in excess of those suggested by its waterline length.

Polyethylene — a thermoplastic used in board manufacture.

Radical — of advanced design (with regard to equipment) or considerable difficulty (with regard to manoeuvre).

Rails — the sides of the board.

Reaching — a point of sailing roughly across the wind.

Rig — a general term describing the mast, sail and boom, as a total entity.

Roach — the area of the leech beyond a line from clew to head supported by battens.

Running — sailing with the wind from aft (behind).

Set — the fine trim of the sail.

Shaper — a person who shapes custom boards.

Sinker — a board that will not support the sailor's weight when not in motion.

Skeg — the fin that gives directional stability.

Spin out — the fin losing its grip, causing the board to lose directional stability.

Tacking — turning the nose of the board up and through the eye of the wind.

Tail — the rear section of the board.

Universal joint — the connection between mast-foot and mast base (usually rubber).

Uphaul — a piece of rope used to lift the sail out of the water.

Index

Additional photographs supplied by Alex Badley, Gary Gibson and Eddie Harper.